Book endorsements

Grief is powerful and universal. It is something we all experience at some point in our lives. Yet most of us are poorly equipped to deal with it effectively. This book is about to change that. Georgena has delivered a masterpiece—a powerhouse combination of raw, emotional real life experience and practical, tested personal tools for transforming grief into the powerful teacher that it is. As with any emotional journey—you have to feel it, to heal it. This book will help you do both.

Rev. Dr. David F. Alexander D.D.
Leadership Council Chair, Centers for Spiritual Living

Grief lives in the body. <u>A New Mourning:Discovering the Gifts in Grief</u> illuminates the power of the Rubenfeld Synergy Method® to be the headlight through grief. When light is brought to the darkness of grief through listening touch and compassionate dialogue, grief is dissipated. Georgena has generously shared her emotional journey through the unimaginable grief of losing her child to finding new joy and gratitude in life. Let her be your Grief Guide. There is none like her.

Noël Wight, Co-Director
Rubeneld Synergy Training Institute

"If you're in the grip of grief, read this book! G............ntly guide you with deep love and fierce ·............................ ιod make peace possible, even now, even

Raphael Cushnir, author of *The* .... *Unleashing the Power of Emotional Connectio.*

A New Mourning:
Discovering the Gifts in Grief

Brandy,

May this book be a Light in the Vortex of your Grief.

Peace and Blessings,

Georgena Eggleston

Georgena

BALBOA.
PRESS
A DIVISION OF HAY HOUSE

Holy Bible-New Revised Standard Version Copyright- 1989, by the Division of Christian Education of theNational Coucil of Churches of Christ in the United States of America. Published by Thoma Nelson,Inc.,Nashville,TN 37214

Balboa Press books may be ordered through booksellers or by contacting:

Balboa Press
A Division of Hay House
1663 Liberty Drive
Bloomington, IN 47403
www.balboapress.com
1 (877) 407-4847

Print information available on the last page.

ISBN: 978-1-5043-3028-2 (sc)
ISBN: 978-1-5043-3030-5 (hc)
ISBN: 978-1-5043-3029-9 (e)

Library of Congress Control Number: 2015904705

Balboa Press rev. date: 06/09/2015

This book is dedicated to my son,
Vincent Edward Eggleston,
for his wisdom as my teacher,
his persistence as a screenwriter, and
his goodness as human being

Contents

❧◎ ◎◈

Foreword

❧ ◦❧

I met Georgena Eggleston in one of my workshops at the Omega Institute in Rhinebeck, New York, in May 1998. She came into the workshop looking all put-together. However, her body was a bundle of raw nerves swimming in my hug! I sensed an overwhelming sadness and shame in her soma (body). Georgena introduced herself as a speech pathologist. As she spoke, this was obvious to all who were in the room.

I slowly guided the participants through a body-mind exercise. They all lay on the floor and followed my directions and my metaphors. Georgena struggled through all of this. She did her best, looking around at others for assurances that she was "doing it right."

I ended the workshop a bit early because some people had to make a train. Georgena was very anxious that she would miss hers. I appreciated her "anxiety" about making connections home, and I gave her an especially long hug as she left. I knew that this person would be supported through her grief with the power of *The Rubenfeld Synergy Method*®! (RSM is an integration of body, mind, emotions, and spirit)

As I predicted, Georgena became a trainee in my Rubenfeld Synergy Training program (RST). She was quick to volunteer for a Rubenfeld Synergy session and made her way to the table. At the end of the session, I gave her my honest and positive feedback. "Your observational skills are valid—not only for others, but for yourself." As I said this, my eyes, ears, and hands were releasing a great deal of trauma from her body and restoring a sense of *confidence* that grieving people rarely give to themselves. She named her Rubenfeld Synergy session "Knee to Life," which provided her with the grounding that was so necessary. Georgena began to feel and trust her body as an ally through her grief.

In this book, Georgena has given you precious tools to heal yourself. The exercises at the end of many chapters are simple and powerful.

They have been experienced personally by Georgena. Each chapter and exercise is a treasure! It has the *potential* of bringing you closer to your *body* and supporting you through your grief!

By asking a family member (or a friend) to assist, you will be offering them a unique opportunity to accompany you through your *grief* process.

Georgena's courage, self-disclosure, and life-changing discoveries are worth every tear for you as the reader. Her writing will move you—it did me! If you have never experienced a *loss* that has brought you to your knees—read this book! This book will be your "life-preserver" when you experience a wave of grief! No one has to drown in grief again. *The Body Tells The Truth,* and it is a powerful way through grief into a new beginning.

This book is a must-read for every "talk" therapist and every Rubenfeld Synergist!
Ilana Rubenfeld, PhD
Creator of the Rubenfeld Synergy Method®,
Author of *The Listening Hand,* published by
Bantam Press.

Preface

I was drowning in grief. My mind was like a top spinning with *if only, why didn't I,* and simply, *why?* I flailed as I resisted my feelings of overwhelming sadness and despair. Grief stabbed my left shoulder. I did not know that grief lives in one's body or that curiosity and self-care were tools to support me to move beyond my grief.

This book was written to share my voyage, bring grief to light, and share four powerful tools that support people on the inevitable journey through grief that awaits us all as human beings.

A short, quick read, the book is intended to support you, the reader. You may be a person deep in the vortex of grief, someone who wants to wisely bear witness to the grief of another, or a seeker looking ahead to the time when grief might descend upon the tapestry of your life. Or, you might be a professional therapist or Synergist who will provide this book as a resource to clients. Then again, you may be hoping to support a loved one who is grieving.

As I trained to become a trauma specialist employing the Rubenfeld Synergy Method®, the grief that lived in my body was released. Many times, it was simple, quick, and painless. Other times, the sessions were intense. I knew that this method, which taught the concepts of curiosity and self-care, was needed by our nation. Now, my dream as a Grief Guide is to teach others to acknowledge and work through grief, especially for those touched by suicide.

This book would never have come into your hands without the guidance of my skillful editor, Christi Krug. The thoughtful feedback of Valerie Koch, Noel Wight, Beth Nelson, and Ilana Rubenfeld helped the book become user-friendly. I'm grateful for the encouragement of my son, Vincent, who told me to write the truth and not be concerned about anything else. I also appreciate the skillful questions and insights of professionals: Holly Duckworth, Ted Norton, David Lacka, Tom Zuba, Shariff Abdullah and the Reverend Shannon O'Hurley, who supported the emergence of so many wonderful concepts. Further, my deepest gratitude goes to Mary Lynn Schaffer, Barb Golden, Judith Maurer, Patt Boatman, Sherry Johnson, Kandace Pile, Kris Scheer, Pam Sears, Bob and Kristie Smith, Diane Marie Blinn, Chris Walker, Kay Whipple, Gayle Ellis, Patricia Orphanidis, Alan Kuzma, Patricia Doane, Peggy Hinrichs, Edward Eggleston, and my friends and family who held me in love in my Raw and Fragile Grief states. Thanks to Carolyn Winkler, Tory Thompson, Ken and Glyndon Ruth Kimbrough, and Edye Allen for holding the vision of this book while it was written in Portland.

Introduction

G rief is the deep, dark, feelings and thoughts that occur as a natural consequence of loss. We must feel it in our heart and body to heal it. Grief lives in the body, choking the life force and constricting peace and freedom.

This book introduces you to the power of Mindful Grieving and Intentional Mourning. It empowers you, as a grieving person, in whatever type of grief you are in, to mourn intentionally. If you are someone who has not yet had a major loss, it gives you the *why* of Mindful Grieving. If you know someone who is grieving, you may put it in their hands with, "I don't know what to say to comfort you, but this woman does." If you are a Rubenfeld Synergist, this book demonstrates the power of the method in my transformational process through grief. If you are a professional working with grieving people, it gives you four tools to support your clients:

1. Awareness that discovery and curiosity about the gifts in grief can lighten grief.
2. Awareness that the body holds one's grief as well as a method to release it.
3. The knowledge that self-care is the foundation for moving beyond your grief into self-love.
4. Tools to replace longing with a new love connection using object permanence as Oneness.

Have you ever had a flat tire that stopped you from driving your car? You either called someone to change it for you, or you put on the spare tire yourself. Either way, there was a tool kit to change the flat tire. Since every one of us is going to experience grief in this lifetime, wouldn't it be wise to have the tools to move through grief and not be flattened by it?

This book is for anyone who wants new tools to move beyond grief.

Mindful Grieving teaches people about Raw, Fragile, and Gentle Grief; the myths that keep us flattened like that tire; and the tools of awareness and curiosity to navigate the tsunami of emotions that pull us down into the vortex of grief.

Mindful Grieving invites the awareness that grief will be transformative. We may enter grief as a mess and emerge in a new life we had no idea existed for us. It is as if we enter the cocoon of grief like a caterpillar. After the caterpillar eats and eats, it spins a cocoon and then turns to soup. It is no longer recognizable. We, too, turn to soup, no longer recognizable to ourselves when we are grieving. In the natural cycle, scientists have discovered "imaginal cells," glimpses of the butterfly-to-be floating in that caterpillar soup. Trusting that we will move through and beyond this grief, we recognize imaginal cells as lights to guide us so we, too, can emerge as the butterfly, a reinvention of ourselves. Mindful Grieving teaches us to bring resources into the vortex of grief, with confidence, so grief becomes a transformative process instead of one that stunts our growth.

Intentional Mourning moves the deep, dark feelings and thoughts out of our bodies. When we intentionally mourn, the tools of gratitude, discovery, curiosity, and self-care create moments of kindness, love, and even joy in the midst of this dark cocoon of grief. Intentional Mourning supports the grieving person to choose those actions that move them beyond grief back into aliveness. The thoughts and feelings we resist persist. Rather, Intentional Mourning invites the body to become an ally in the grief process, recognizing that the body is not merely something we drag around but a fount of resources to strengthen and guide us through grief. Intentional Mourning can be the catalyst to reinvent ourselves so we are not stuck for the rest of our lives. It nutures the confidence that we can choose how this transformational process is going to look.

Grief is the anguished feelings and thoughts that flood over us after a loss. Fear grips us in grief. The initial Raw Grief is when the tsunami swells of shock, disbelief, anger, and sadness seemingly come out of nowhere, sending us to the depths of despair. This grief cocoons our brains in a fog so dense and dark that we can barely see our way. In Raw Grief, everything and everyone in our life is seen through the lens of moment-by-moment grief. It is as if grief has spilled over the tapestry of our lives. Grief is the only thing visible.

Fragile Grief occurs when our brain begins to function once again. But we feel like a dragon is draggin' us around. In this grief, we keep thinking the same thoughts, which trigger feelings of anger, hatred, sadness, frustration, guilt, and even shame. The tapestry of our life has a rough, rope-like thread that is evident to everyone who meets us. Fragile Grief may last years—or the rest of our lives. The choice is ours.

Gentle Grief is the relief that, just as the sun comes up every morning, we have stepped into a New Mourning. It is like the deer moving into sight at the edge of the clearing. The thread of grief continues in the tapestry of our lives, but it is now part of who we are. It becomes a subtle thread in fabric of our lives.

In this book, you will discover where grief lived in my body and see the power of the Rubenfeld Synergy Method®, which released it and replaced the old beliefs, attitudes, and behaviors with self-acceptance and self-love. It helped me soften and become a kinder, gentler me.

You will discover that the developmental process of object permanence is eternal Oneness. Even when the ball rolls behind the couch, the toddler learns that it is not lost. At that moment, the toddler has acquired object permanence. The concept of "where is the one I love?" will be explored.

Many of the self-care strategies that helped my Intentional Mourning are shared throughout this book. Over time, my curiosity expanded, my heart lightened, and I began to float above the many fears triggered by the loss of my son, Reed.

You will read how suicide is now occurring more gently and Reed's experience of it on the other side. His after-death communications gave us relief and peace.

To the professionals who will embrace this book to support clients in a new way of being, I thank you. To each of you who has never felt the tsunami of grief and are choosing to read this book, you have my deepest gratitude for loving yourself enough to be proactive. For those in my Synergy community, here is the book you have been requesting.

How I wish you, the Grieving One, were in a place where this book was not needed. I know the heart, mind, and gut-wrenching pain of grief. You have my profound compassion, empathy, and admiration for the progress you have made that brought you to this place of holding *A New Mourning* in your hands.

Georgena Eggleston
Portland, OR
October 6, 2014

PART I

The Gifts in Raw Grief Appear

Discovering a New Calling

───────────────── ❧ ❧ ─────────────────

Gathered outside the emergency room, we all waited for a miracle.

Inside the pale-yellow waiting room, I felt my heart somersaulting. In contrast to the cell of a room at the high school, which our family had escaped earlier, this place was huge. I felt lost, free-floating. Unable to sit, I wandered into a hallway.

There was Tom Surber, a physician and a friend of many years. Grateful to find someone who could do something, I rushed to meet him.

"Tom, we have to get Reed out of here on Life Flight to a pediatric neurosurgeon in Omaha." I knew it was the only way my ninth-grade son would survive his injuries.

Tom's face was grim. "Georgena, fog has just blanketed the area. Life Flight can't fly in to get him. Even if they could, Reed's going to die."

His words expressed what I knew in my mother's heart. Based on my experience working as a speech-language pathologist at Shock Trauma in Baltimore, I knew the long road back from a severe head injury to an independent life. Few made the trip successfully. Even if Reed did survive, his life would be full of hardships.

Tom hugged me, and the first tears began gushing from my heart. Turning away to compose myself, I realized in a wave of relief that my brilliant son Reed wouldn't face rehabilitation.

Carried by a force beyond myself, I sought the solace of a far-off corner of the hallway. Yet as I retreated to my spot, I saw a huddle of three authorities from my son's school. There was Lee, a teddy bear of a man, slumped forward in his raincoat, oozing exhaustion. As the junior high

3

principal, he had announced to my son that evening that he had failed his breathalyzer test. Lee's eyes were downcast. He was silent.

It was a surprise to see Chad, the director of student services. Chad knew his job well as the policies and procedures authority in our Midwestern public school system. Standing ramrod straight, he addressed the other two men. His thin, furrowed face revealed his type-A personality. I couldn't hear what he was saying or use my lip-reading skills. My mind was in too much of a blur.

Tim, the senior high principal, thrust his hands in his pockets and fixed his eyes on his superior, listening intently. It was at Tim's school that Reed had attended what would be his last basketball game.

The three stood at attention as I approached. "Reed's going to die," I heard myself saying. "We've got to get these kids safely through this trauma and their grief." A commanding presence unfolded from my own words.

The others looked at me in complete shock that this could be happening. The color drained from their faces. Tim gasped, and Lee turned away. Chad looked at me and said nothing.

Stepping back, I felt somehow empowered. Within me there was neither contempt nor anger for any of them. We were thrust together, mother and men, to support the hundreds of teenagers now reeling from the aftermath of a single shotgun blast.

Words came through me that would determine the rest of my life's work. In that moment, I became a trauma specialist, a grief guide. I didn't have a moment to ponder this role, and I didn't realize what I'd undertaken. It would be years before a coaching session would focus all of my certifications, spiritual tools, and personality quirks into a calling I could no longer avoid.

In that moment at the hospital, the courage, faith, and urgency to guide Reed's friends through grief's grip moved through every fiber of my being. I stepped into the certitude that this challenge was mine to embrace. I hoped that these men could and would join me in that challenge.

I didn't realize the scope of all that I would come to learn about grief—that grief could be a catalyst for growth and transformation, and that one can move through grief and beyond with a sense of discovery and return to feeling alive and joyful.

I didn't know that the body is instrumental in this process or that when a loved one passes, trauma invades the body, lodging there as grief. I didn't know about raw grief, fragile grief, or gentle grief. I didn't have training in mindful grief or intentional mourning. I had experienced the anticipatory grief of my mother's death and dipped into the vortex of grief when my brother, father-in-law, and father departed. Like most people in our culture, I was totally unprepared for grief.

One must feel grief to heal from it. To hear one's heart and discern its guidance, the mind must be still, and the body must be heard with a gentle, listening touch. I didn't know there were many gifts in my embodied trauma and grief. Yet I did feel a sense of courage, an innate faith, and curiosity.

I would soon discover that I had a choice. I could effectively release my embodied trauma and transcend grief, or I could move through my mourning in a tedious journey that would be as painful and arduous as a climbing a mountain.

Turning from the three men, I sought my husband, Edward. "We can't Life Flight Reed to Omaha," I reported stoically. "Tom said Reed's going to die." My strong voice was now barely a whisper as I once again voiced my son's fate.

Edward didn't reply. It was he who had seen Reed's body enfolded in the camouflage hunting coat, his face a bloody pool, the shotgun lying on the cement floor, brain tissue and blood spattering the walls. It was Edward who smelled the gunpowder as he cradled his son. It was he who knew the moment his eyes took in the scene that Reed's soul was gone.

Holding his son's warm body, Edward knew that Reed's life force, his essence, had departed. It would be months before he could put those moments into words.

As Edward and I wrapped our arms around each other, tears streamed down my face.

Even though Lee, the junior high principal, and I had been together just one night earlier, it seemed like a thousand ages in the past. Lee and I had met in the home of Greg and Pam Sears, who were pillars in our church. We all served on the Christian Education committee of our local United Church of Christ. I was the senior high Sunday school teacher. My son Vincent and the Searses' daughter, Lindsey, were seniors.

"Could we change Sunday school to Sunday night?" Pam had proposed as we tried to find strategies to help our youth. "Sunday morning could be the only morning these kids have to sleep in."

As a mainline Protestant denomination, we didn't yet have the draw of a praise band during our Sunday morning service. Doughnuts and parental prodding were the main motivations for our teens to haul themselves out of bed and arrive at nine on a Sunday morning to receive spiritual tools to help them navigate the turbulent waters of adolescence. We knew our teens were scheduled to the max.

A lively discussion ensued. Susan Surber, Tom's wife, had two sons in the high school class as well. "I second this new thought," she said. "I certainly don't like waking the boys to get them to church every Sunday morning."

We knew we had the power to support our children with this simple act.

"Let's poll the kids, and if they vote for it, we'll change the schedule. We must care for our kids. If there's one thing I learned in Shock Trauma, it's that we just never know …" My voice trailed off as the scene of a bloody, mangled teenaged body on a gurney floated into my awareness. I had witnessed such tragedies in my work many times. It reminded me that life could change in an instant.

There was the woman who had eaten shellfish on her anniversary and suffered a fatal brain-stem aneurism hours later. She had been younger than I was. There had also been the radiant brunette who had been thrown from a car and who was paralyzed from the neck down. These individuals had simply been enjoying life. They weren't doing anyone harm, just living in the moment. But their lives had changed forever.

These experiences reminded me to be grateful for all the little things in life, such as the warmth of Pam and Greg's home that evening. Heat is a luxury for many Americans.

When the meeting adjourned, I excused myself, my mouth watering for Pam's apple pie. But I felt drawn to leave early and have a Coke with Reed, my fifteen-and-a-half-year-old gifted student. Looking back, I sensed that my soul somehow knew that the end to the life I had known was imminent.

Descending the steps to the basement that Thursday night, I saw him as I had seen him so often: head bent intently over the paper in front of him. In the past, he'd sat like that to sketch his favorite athletes, Cal Ripken and Michael Jordan. That night, he was focused on a math problem. His jaw was clenched, and he seemed engrossed in homework, not even glancing up to check the basketball game on the screen in front of him.

"Hi, Reed. Want to take a break and have a Coke?"

He had just begun drinking pop again after putting himself on a six-month fast during his cross-country training and competition.

"Leave me alone! I have to figure this problem out."

I was stunned and retreated up the stairs. *Where had this rage come from?* He hadn't been upset when I picked him up from ninth-grade basketball practice. He'd been fine at dinner.

A gifted mathematician, he was the one kids turned to for a fresh explanation to a problem. He was consistently on the honor roll, as he was a perfectionist. That night, he was demonstrating his need to be left alone when things weren't going well.

Friday morning, Reed seemed his usual self. As the day rolled into evening, my family kicked back for pizza in the living room. Usually, we gathered around our heirloom oak table and shared the day's events. But this night, we were happy to take it easy, grateful for comfort food and our time together.

Vincent, a high school senior, headed up to his room to read *The Perfect Storm.* He was taking his SATs the next morning to secure his appointment to the Merchant Marine Academy. This sensitive, shy soul would soon be driving ships for the military.

My father, George, a veteran had been so proud when Vincent received the news.

Edward headed off to the basement to watch the News Hour. We had laughingly agreed as a couple when Vincent was born that I would raise our children until age twelve and after that, Edward would take over. He was much more easygoing than I. We knew that our children needed the safety of boundaries to establish their roots. They also needed trust, support, and freedom to give them wings. Our temperaments were well matched to work together in all of this.

Edward could see the big picture and yet make detailed arrangements, such as those needed for Vincent's summer school and Reed's science camp. We were fortunate to agree on parental roles.

After the last bite of pizza had disappeared, Reed met me at the kitchen sink. He smiled. "Aren't you going to scrub the kitchen floor?"

"Are you expecting company?" I said. I knew he was thinking of his girlfriend as he smiled that smile that could brighten every darkness.

"Sure am. We need to get Allison about 7:30. Will you mix some orange juice?"

"Help me load the dishwasher, and you can clean the guest bathroom while I scrub the floor."

We each set to work to complete our tasks. There was no appearance of the anger and frustration I'd seen the night before—just a fifteen-and-a-half-year-old boy charming his mother.

As we drove through the bitter cold of that starlit night to pick up Allison, I suddenly felt my fatigue. I wasn't sure what prompted my next words. "If anything ever happened to me," I began.

Reed looked at me with a flash of worry and then looked away.

"... I know you and Vincent would be fine," I finished.

Reed erupted. "How can you say such a thing? Haven't we had enough death in this family? Grandma Betty and Granddad George haven't even been gone six months."

We drove on in silence.

When Allison got in the car, her chattiness engaged Reed. She was a new girlfriend, not from his middle school crowd.

"So what are you doing while your parents are gone?" he asked.

"Well, I'm staying with my grandmother tonight. Mom and Dad won't be back from Hawaii for ten days. So tomorrow, Brittany's mom will pick me up. We'll all eat at the mall and try on gowns for Winter Royalty."

Reed shrugged. "But we can't go to the dance as ninth graders."

Allison giggled. "That won't stop us from trying on the gowns!"

Soon, laughter from the backseat washed away my concern over Reed's anger.

As we walked into the house, the winter wind wedged through a slit of my down coat. In the kitchen, Reed and Allison stopped to retrieve the orange juice out of the fridge. They headed upstairs to his room. They left the door open, in keeping with the family rule.

I settled at the heirloom oak table to pay bills. When I glanced at the clock, I felt a sense of unease. Just above my head was all this hormonal energy. Climbing the stairs, I had an agenda.

Allison was sitting at the head of the bed, propped on pillows. Reed sat cross-legged at the foot of the bed, his back unsupported. It was a metaphor I would later recall, wondering how I'd missed it.

A "Tickle Me Elmo" sat between them. Allison and Reed took turns pulling its string and laughing at the silly sayings. She'd given it to Reed for Christmas.

The sexual tension in the air was now palpable. I reached for a solution. "Aren't you going to the basketball game?"

"We're thinkin' about it," Reed replied.

One did not push Reed. He pushed himself. But I felt an urgency to get them out of the house and around their peers. Even though the door was open, I did not have the tools to deal with hot hormones. Not tonight.

"The game has already started. Dad can take you."

"All right, we'll go."

In agreeing to go to the game, Reed would no longer feel the support of his family and friends. Each sentence he would hear and each person he would encounter would sever his connection to the supportive life he knew. His shame would sentence him to a single option.

Reed's fateful choice would end his life.

We hugged good-bye for the second time that day. An "I love you" hug was the way we departed every morning. And yet there was something I missed. I didn't get a good look in the dim entryway. I did not see Reed's glassy eyes as they all stepped out into the frigid night.

The Shame of Losing Face
FRIDAY, JANUARY 23, 1998

A lone in the house, I stepped outside to brace myself against the ever-stronger wind and place the paid bills in the mailbox by the driveway.

Edward was home within minutes, as we were less than a mile from the high school.

"Want to watch ESPN with me?" Edward asked. Still shivering, I nodded, as the idea of cuddling on the couch sounded lovely.

I followed Edward downstairs, soon lulled by the action of the screen before me. I jumped when the phone rang. Was there no peace?

I finally came to my senses on the third ring. I mounted the stairs by twos.

"Georgena, this is Lee. Please come to the school. We think Reed's been drinking."

"Drinking? But he was upstairs in his room!" My mind was spinning. But before I could take the next breath, I blurted, "We'll be right there."

"Vincent!" I called up the stairs. "Your father and I are going to the high school. I just got a call. They think Reed's been drinking."

"Have him take the breathalyzer test," came Vincent's immediate reply. "It will tell the truth."

My sense of responsibility took over. We had always been a family that followed the rules. I knew that Vincent drank, as well as other athletes in our town. That was something I accepted—older athletes were often drinkers. But now, Reed? He was only fifteen and a half.

Instantaneously, I felt the ability to act, despite the fear that gripped me. I was not powerless. Yet I didn't take the time to go into Reed's room or discover my dad's bottle of vodka under the bed. I was in a rush to get to the school. To comply with the authorities. I did not take a moment to learn the truth for myself or figure out how to soften the frustration for my son. I did not check in with my body because I did not know how.

I went into White Rabbit mode. *I'm late. I'm late for a very important date.* It was my go-to reaction when I felt the need to control what was happening around me. My tightly wound nervous system thrust me into panic.

It was this rushed buildup of internal pressure that I had learned as a sensitive child. I had to fix things. Those in authority had to be soothed.

Tonight it was the school authorities I was responding to.

"What do you want to do, Edward?" I asked as we drove. We had to think fast over this single-mile journey.

"The breathalyzer will certainly tell the truth," was his wise reply.

"If Reed fails the test, you can be sure I'll be at the front door of the Eppley Center in Omaha on Monday morning with both Vincent and Reed." My throat tightened. "What happened with Mark at least taught us about addiction. I refuse to let alcohol trigger the horrific events that it did for my brother."

For a moment, I felt like a strong mother bear, ready to protect her young ones in their need. Yet in the next moment, the fearful White Rabbit showed up, seeking to appease the authorities.

Once at the school, we were ushered into a tiny fishbowl of a room with a large window. Lee, the junior high principal, sat behind a wooden desk, and Reed sat nearby.

"Hello," we each greeted Lee.

Reed didn't look at us.

"Reed, you were pulled out of the game tonight," began Lee, "because of who you were with."

We would later learn that several kids had been pulled out and questioned. Allison was among those given the breathalyzer test. Yet her grandmother was not called.

Lee knew that Reed had a charismatic influence on his peers and needed to be dealt with differently. And so he called us in and requested our consent.

"Were you drinking?" I asked Reed, looking him in the eye and keeping my voice even. I had to ask this question. In this moment I felt strong, objective, and ready to listen to him. We were here to discover the truth, however heartbreaking.

"No," came the soft reply, and Reed turned his eyes briefly on Edward and me.

As a speech-language pathologist, I was attuned to voice quality. The hollowness of Reed's "no" revealed the truth—that indeed, he *had* been drinking. But I was not really listening. The mother bear of protection in me had disappeared completely now, overshadowed by fear as the White Rabbit took over.

How often do we fail as parents to see what is before us? Our blind spots are destructive. Unhealthy patterns disconnect us from ourselves and those we love most.

I sighed. "Just take the test then, Reed, and it will prove your innocence." I was thinking ahead to the rocky-road of alcohol rehab that might very well be next.

"Okay." He gulped and then said, "But I did take some mouthwash. Will that make me guilty?"

The principal stood up. "I will get the off duty officer. Wait here." He left the room.

I looked over at my teenage son. Head down, learning forward into clenched hands, artist's hands that had created so much beauty in only fifteen years.

I had just sentenced this gifted, sensitive, popular child to a tsunami of embarrassment and shame.

As I'd learn from the kids later, Reed was the next one who would put Norfolk, Nebraska on the map. Johnny Carson, the first famous resident, had referred to this Midwestern town numerous times during his years hosting *The Tonight Show*.

Reed's peers all looked up to him. They saw his giftedness, and as they finished their art projects, they would each in turn gaze on his. In fifth grade, he drew a butterfly wing that would grace a PTA postcard. He inspired his ninth-grade basketball team with timely exhortations.

He was always the last to leave practice, determined to perfect his extra point shot. He never failed at what he put his mind to.

Reed was a determined leader, a champion for the underdog, and one who always saw the best in others. Yet he only saw the worst in himself.

Edward sat silent. His jaw was tightly clenched, his eyes were cast downward. He and Reed were opposites. Reed was expected to attend Harvard, Brown, or the Air Force Academy. These were places off-limits to Edward because of his upbringing. Despite his brilliant mind, Edward had been denied entrance into Stanford. He had not had the guidance necessary to leap from a tiny Nebraska high school to a first-tier university. He wanted better for his sons. Just the weekend before, Edward had taken Vincent to New York to tour the Merchant Marine Academy. He knew they could have the world.

And now I was headed into the most devastating hour of my life, totally unaware of what it would come. A profound calm enveloped me. I felt safety and unconditional love.

Neither Reed nor Edward moved. Yet I relaxed back into my chair and allowed my breath to deepen. I felt the supporting arms of a Presence beyond myself. I was held, safe and protected.

Years later, I would offer these same qualities to my grieving clients.

"I had a beer in the shower after practice, and we were drinking orange juice and vodka in my room," Reed volunteered. His voice was soft, full of regret. Shame pulled at his face. The life drained from his eyes.

Good. Reed had told us the truth. He was not perfect, and tonight he would once again be too hard on himself, angry, as perfectionists often are.

In the days to come, I would need to remember that I had been a good parent. I had succeeded in instilling the values of honesty, responsibility, courage, and discipline in each of my sensitive, gifted sons.

I looked lovingly at Reed. *We all make mistakes*, I thought. *I was at peace. I did not sense the terror in my son. I did not spring into action, block the door, and order Edward to take Reed to safety.* I simply sat, enfolded in this Peaceful Presence, my heart moving out to my beloved son.

For the last five years, mine had been a journey to live in love. I was seeking to see and know God in all circumstances. The sermons in church, the Bible study, the daily devotions, all helped me to hold myself to a new level of consciousness. I was motivated to live with the eyes of love for everyone and everything—yet I always excluded myself. Tonight, for the first time in my life, I felt this limitless sea of unconditional love.

The officer strode in, thrusting the breathalyzer toward Reed, who was sitting at attention.

"Blow," he demanded. He mumbled the reading, turned the screen toward the principal, and disappeared down a hallway.

"Reed," said the principal as he pointed a finger at the young man sitting in front of him, "you are off the ninth grade basketball team for the rest of the year. And you're suspended from school for three days."

Lee shook his head and rose wearily from his desk, disappearing after the police officer.

We were alone.

Edward slammed his fist on the desk. "No tolerance for kids, they keep saying. Why are kids held to a higher standard than drunken professionals with multiple DWIs? This town is full of hypocrites!" He gritted his teeth.

Edward had met with the school board members last fall to protest their "no tolerance" rule. Several were our friends who had their own teens in the soccer program Edward had up-leveled and expanded. The board's black-and-white thinking simply did not allow for listening to kids or struggling alongside them to help them find healthy patterns.

Edward knew that his teenage son was like a butterfly. Strong enough to fly hundreds of miles, yet possessing transparent wings so fragile they were easily torn. He opened the door across from Reed and strode from the room, seething at this injustice.

Alone with Reed, I spoke out with a soft tone. "We will get through this, Reed. Remember, every problem has a manageable solution."

My intention that night was one of correction, as the responsible parent who teaches that choices have consequences.

I paused. "I'm going to find your girlfriend," I said, standing close to him. He slumped forward, silent, hands covering the shame on his face. There was no sigh. Hardly a breath moved through him.

I made the fatal assumption that he heard me.

We did not have then the brain scan studies that now show how every negative word, sour facial expression, or harsh tone of voice excites the listener's amygdala, sending danger signals throughout the brain. The listening centers in our temporal lobes shut down, the logic centers of the frontal lobe are derailed, and the empathy circuits in our insula turn off.

I hesitated, hoping Reed would look up or do something to show he wasn't turning inward, as was his pattern when angry. Lately, I had learned to give him space to cool off, to figure things out in peace and quiet. This had been my strategy the night before when he had struggled over math.

I did not touch him then; I did not take his hand in mine. I did not realize that this problem would have a tragic solution. I did not read his soul.

I found Allison isolated in another tiny room. Her light-brown hair was glommed onto her tear-stained cheeks. She jumped up and sobbed, "My parents are going to be so mad at me!" I walked over to offer a comforting embrace.

Her body softened as I hugged her. "We all make mistakes," I soothed. When I stepped back, I gently asked her to look at me.

"You are forgiven," I said, looking into her eyes. "You are a good person." With loving kindness, I wiped the mascara from her face and held her for the long while before her grandmother arrived.

The Peaceful Presence now moved through me, connecting me to the earth like a towering redwood. I knew how to comfort, to nurture.

Just outside the office, Edward saw Reed through the window. Reed stood with arms outstretched, like Christ on the cross, agony on his face. Edward turned his eyes away. He did not watch as the ninth grade basketball coach went in to meet with his star player.

"Coach, Coach, I am so sorry." Reed said. Then, as if by instinct, he bolted out the nearest door.

The coach met Edward outside a second door. Edward imagined Reed still in the room, working things out in his mind. Yet Reed was running down a hallway, slamming a locker with his fist. He called to his teammates, "I will see you on the basketball court next year!"

Reed dashed from the building. Having lettered as a freshman on the cross-country team just months before, Reed inhaled the mile home in the fierce Nebraska winds.

But something happened. His promise to be back next winter suddenly derailed. Perhaps it was the guilt of the moment or the shock of running into the icy night. This was the first time he had ever initiated his own public failure.

He had added vodka to the orange juice. He had failed the breath test. He had been banned from his beloved basketball team.

He shifted from self-loathing to shame. He began to believe that he was a bad person. That what he'd done was unforgivable. His only way out was self-harm. He would take himself out of life.

Arriving home, Reed entered the side door into the garage. He pulled his hunting coat from its hook and grabbed the shotgun from its place in the corner. Then, striding into the adjacent laundry room he found magic markers in the cabinet drawer. He gathered shotgun shells from the closet. All of these actions mark a quick-thinking young man, not someone allegedly drunk. Returning to the garage, he slammed the door loud enough to alert Vincent on the second floor.

Vincent stepped down and poked his head into the dim garage. He was able to make out Reed, a marker in his hand. "I'll be home in a minute," said Reed.

Vincent noted that the gun and hunting coat were on the floor, removed from their usual corner. He returned to the warmth of the house.

He did not see the message Reed scribbled on the wall in red ink: "I'm sorry, Friends and Family." He signed it, "ReeD," with a heart under his name.

Back at the high school, engaged in conversation, Edward glanced away from Reed's basketball coach. He saw the empty room.

A door stood open. Reed was gone.

Driven by fear, Edward raced home, parked the car in the driveway, and did not open the side door of the garage but rushed on past.

Reed was there, unseen, hunched over his grandfather's shotgun, the barrel in his mouth.

"Where is Reed?" Edward called to Vincent from the entry. The shotgun blast answered.

Having safely entrusted Allison to her grandmother, I searched the offices and then the parking lot for Edward and Reed. Stunned by the bitter cold, with Edward's car missing on that starless January night, I returned to the warmth of the nearly deserted school. "May I use the phone?" I asked Lee. He looked as though he were ready to collapse from the weight of his duties as principal.

He nodded permission.

I picked up the receiver and dialed my home number. The primal wail in my ear did not register in my brain. *What was this high-pitched, unintelligible sound? It sounded like a moan, but not really. Was it made by an animal in pain? It surely was not human.*

I hung up. *Had I dialed the correct number?* Continuing to feel the support and comfort of the Peaceful Presence, I took a deep breath and tried a second time, dialing very slowly. Shaking my head, I mouthed each number. This was in 1998, long before cell phones.

"Mom, come home quick!" Vincent's strangled voice gripped my heart. I had never heard my easygoing son flood the air with such sounds of anxiety.

"Can you take me home?" I asked, turning to Lee. Our church meeting together just twenty-four hours earlier seemed like a lifetime ago.

My calm remained even when I heard the sirens as we stepped toward Lee's car in the darkness. I knew their shrill wails were coming from my house.

"Can we hurry?" was all I said to Lee. Leaning into that powerful Presence, I breathed and prayed. I prayed to be loving-kindness. I prayed to be peace.

I did not know that, years later, I was to be a bringer of that peace and harmony into the midst of chaos. I had no concept of the chaos about to engulf me.

Flashing emergency vehicle lights jolted me back to my usual mode. Focused. Thinking. Doing. Taking charge.

Springing from the car, I inhaled sharply at the scene before me. The trauma of the moment became frozen in my diaphragm.

In that moment, the world began to breathe for me as I disconnected from myself. Air entered my lungs automatically.

My eyes riveted upon the figure of Vincent, leaping up and down on the icy concrete driveway. He was clad in his navy velour jogging suit, his feet bare. Arms flapping, he vainly tried to take flight from the chaos around him. He was screaming in a way I had never seen.

I ran toward him. "Vincent!" I shrieked.

He stopped, unplugged at the sound of his name. He reached for me. He was the last one to see his brother alive. He had heard the gunshot. He had called 911. He wanted to protect me from all of this.

I turned as Reed was being wheeled away on a gurney. The ambu-bag was forcing oxygen into his lungs. Only his upper lip was visible under the white drapes.

I had seen this scene before in Baltimore. But the one beneath the sheets had never been someone I had carried in my womb.

Vincent held me tight.

Breaking away, I searched for Edward. Not finding him, I then turned back to Vincent. "We have to get to the hospital," was all I could say.

Stopping at the side door of the garage, I screamed, seeing the blood on the floor and the policewoman standing there. "This is a crime scene," she said in a shaking voice. "Don't come any closer." Yet just ninety minutes earlier it had been my home.

"This is my home," I said, feeling a surge of ownership and protection. "Don't tell me what to do." It was the mother bear, but she was too late.

The mother bear had not been there to protect Reed when I had realized his guilt.

Discovering the Gift of Exhaustion: Resist or Rest?

SATURDAY, JANUARY 24–WEDNESDAY, JANUARY 28, 1998

~⊙ ⊙~

I was held up through shock, adrenaline, and that Peaceful Presence throughout that last night of Reed's life. I sat or knelt beside Reed's bed holding his right hand all night. I did not climb into bed and hold him as one holds an infant. The thought never occurred to me because I was too "proper" for that, in this hospital setting where everyone knew me in my professional role. At one point, I fell asleep, probably just for an instant. I awoke with the thought, "Oh, I have fallen asleep, just as the disciples did."

An hour before Reed was pronounced dead, we called Tom Guenther to the hospital. He was our minister, and he loved Reed. I wanted Tom to be able to sleep as long as possible because I knew the days ahead would be nearly as grueling for him as for us. Although dressed to the nines, Tom was visibly shaken. Reed had been the one who "got" Tom's sense of adventure. He loved watching Reed return from making mischief to giving his complete attention as a confirmation student. My last touch was holding Reed's hand during Tom's comforting prayer and then kissing it. Saying, "Good-bye. I love you. I am so sorry." (I would later learn that Reed's note on the garage wall was nearly identical.) I turned to Tom. "Will you please take me home? Edward is staying here, waiting for the transplant team driving up from Lincoln."

On the drive home, I told him what I knew. When we reached the house, it was still. I crept upstairs. I could sense Vincent safely asleep in his bed. After he had said a tearful good-bye to his brother, we had allowed our friends the Walkers to take him back home.

Descending the stairs, I smelled the coffee that Tom had made, and I joined him at the table. The sturdy oak supported my elbows as I lifted the cup to my lips.

Mysteriously, I was drawn to stand at the patio door. Dawn's fingers were peeling back the darkness. A sliver of crimson light was dissipating the night.

I turned to Tom. "Just as the sun comes up every morning, surely I will move through this grief and beyond." I did not know how it would happen. I only knew that the faith within me and the Peaceful Presence that once again surrounded me would guide me on my way.

The very next day, Sunday, January 25, the guidance began. We received our first sign that Reed's soul was soaring. It came as a coyote, my symbol of the wailing of Raw Grief.

I was on my hands and knees scrubbing the kitchen floor before the tide of mourners was expected to arrive. I was hoping to deepen my divine connection. It was here, during this everyday sacred task, that the guidance I sought always became most clear to me. Sometimes I wanted to know what to do with a patient who was not progressing from speaking single words to phrases. Other times, I wondered about a nursing home staff member putting a patient at risk for aspiration. Or perhaps I was discerning how to manage Vincent's upcoming graduation reception.

Today it was, *How do I ever make it through this, God?* I collapsed into a fetal position and began to wail my grief. I was feeling grief's grip at last.

Alan, my beloved brother, stood as witness. He had arrived the night before, bringing his ever-protective presence into the vortex of grief. He later said, "A bad day is when you see your sister in a fetal position unable to move because her world has imploded."

Gasping for breath, I found myself lifted from the puddle of tears as I stood to my feet. I noticed the sun beaming through the patio door and turned toward it, seeking solace. I was magnetized to see the unmistakable sign of Reed. A coyote the color of winter-brown grass was crouching on its haunches in the fairway, twenty-five yards from our condominium. Had the primordial wail of my grief drawn it in?

Reed had drawn coyotes since he was six years old. He would bend his slight frame and crew-cut head intently over the page, bringing reality to the precise scenes he imagined. He gave his Aunt Pat a black-and-white drawing of the lone critter on its haunches howling at the moon. It captured her attention. Living in southwestern Colorado, she often heard the animal's piercing bay when she returned from her evening walks. Coyotes became the subject of her scenes on T-shirts, in oil paintings, and hidden in watercolor. For several years, Reed continued to sketch coyotes in chalk, crayon, and pencil. The details grew more complex but were always similar: a full moon shining in the upper left corner; a lone coyote on hind legs with its head thrown back in the lower right. The viewer could almost feel the chilly night air and see the stars distance themselves from the mournful cry.

That morning, the creature's piercing gaze galvanized us as we crept, one by one, to the glass doors and stared into its eyes. It exuded tranquil strength for Edward, Vincent, Alan, and me. Slowly, it stood on all fours, turned south, sauntered ten yards, and swung its body ninety degrees to face us. For several minutes of silence, the Power of Peaceful Presence bound us together, wild creature and people wild with grief.

Then the coyote disengaged its stare, turned its face southward, and trotted off into the trees.

It had been twenty-four hours since Reed's departure.

The Peaceful Presence continued to hold me for the four days leading up to Reed's funeral. Hundreds of friends and family members came from all over Nebraska to say good-bye. Now it was over.

On this Wednesday morning, Vincent was home with us. Friends and family were down in the kitchen making sense of the abundance of food that had flowed in as a form of support. In Nebraska, when someone was in need of love and comforting, food was evidence of caring.

Caring for others was so easy. Our town of 28,000 had a food pantry, a Meals on Wheels organization, and Bright Horizons, a battered women's shelter.

Even though it was only ten in the morning, I had bid the women good-bye to collapse with Edward upstairs in our bed, the bed where Reed was conceived.

I simply had to begin to take care of myself. My bones ached. So great was the weight I felt, I could not put one foot in front of the other.

I had buried my son yesterday because he was dead.

I had not taken his hand.

I was guilty.

Every cell in my body screamed. I was too tired to cry. I could not take a deep breath. It would be years before the non-invasive trauma of arriving home that Friday night would be released from my frozen diaphragm. This embodied trauma known as grief would take years for me to recognize and release because I did not know that grief lives in one's body. I was not yet attuned to it.

Now in this moment, lying on my bed, exhaustion was all I knew of myself.

I no longer resisted. Sweet sleep rolled in like fog. When I awakened, Edward was gone and the clock said two o'clock. Four hours had disappeared, just like my son.

I took a painful, sharp breath, jolted into tearful longing.

It was my reality: Reed was gone. Tears streamed from my eyes, flowing from my wounded heart.

Where was the Grief Guide who could assure me that Raw Grief would dissipate in as few as ninety days? That the crying for days would give way to crying for hours? That the crying for hours would become crying for minutes? I needed to hear that even the crying for minutes would become seconds, and a new "me" would emerge. But there was no way I could know this.

There was no map through grief's grip. No teacher to show that this initial phase, Raw Grief, is like a tsunami dashing us into the depths of despair. I would later define grief as internal, deep, dark, anguished feelings and thoughts. It's a force that seems to come out of nowhere. The truth is that a thought will trigger grief. One of the things I would learn is that these feelings do not last forever. They move in and out of the depths of our being. The sooner we learn to "dance" with them through the tools of dialogue and gentle Listening Touch, the more rapidly they dissipate. I began to learn Listening Touch ten months later. It occurs as I rub my hands together and bring them apart until I can't feel the heat or energy between them. It feels like I am pulling taffy. I bring them back together and rub them again until the heat/energy returns.

Now, I float one or more hands onto that place or those places in my body calling for attention. My left shoulder is usually aching because this is where grief is living in me.

I am present to myself. I simply notice what is happening beneath my hands. There is no right or wrong answer. I suspend self-judgment, one of the benefits of this gentle, miraculous process of Listening Touch.

We fear that we will never stop crying. By learning to gently, mindfully touch the part of our body that is calling for attention and hearing its messages, the fear vanishes. To willingly listen to yourself, not in words, the feelings of anger, sadness, despair, hopelessness, and fear are given a voice. The process is like riding a roller coaster through the ups and downs of grief. Awareness and gratitude are lights through the darkness. There are moments when to simply have clean underwear and be grateful for it is a gift.

When I had kissed the head and feet of my beloved son for the last time, through his coffin, hope drained out of my body into the ground. *Was my hope buried with him? Would it ever return?*

I must find Vincent, I decided. What was happening with him? I peeled myself from the bed into a sitting position, wrapping the blanket around me. I rose and began my search through the house.

He was safe. He was watching a cooking show, taking in visions of the living element of food. Cooking was another form of his creativity.

I sat and watched with him in silence.

Vincent would tell me years later that he had given up being the artist so that his brother's art could shine. How was it that Vincent believed there could only be one star? How often as parents do we fail to see the formation of beliefs that shape the behaviors of our children?

In the months to come, each time my bones ached, I would sit down or sleep. After major surgery less than two years earlier, I had slept for the entire six-week recovery period. Once again, I could no longer resist my exhaustion. Grief gave way to sleep. The deep REM sleep and naps provided relief.

I had always been one of those driven women who thought she could do it all. I played each role to the max, with my role as a mom as the basis of all my other choices. Baking cookies and ironing my sons' T-shirts were my ways of saying, "I love you." I scheduled everything around the times the boys were home. I read all the "How to be a super mom" articles in the eighties and nineties. Each validated my expertise as a time manager, as I pushed myself to cram more into my days.

Now I was exhausted, not only by my grief over Reed but by the belief that I should not be tired. I didn't know that I could question this belief. I could have asked: *Is this supporting me? Is this belief adding to guilt and exhaustion?*

A Grief Guide gives permission to take the first thirty, sixty, ninety or more days off. This also gives grievers permission to put life on hold for the year of "firsts" without their beloved. Moving through grief involves simply being. Allowing the fatigue, the overwhelm, the roller coaster of feelings. One learns to surrender in each moment by simply floating within the feelings instead of thrashing against them like a drowning woman.

I played the part of the drowning woman. I didn't know how to allow, to surrender, to float instead of fight. Resistance to feeling the feelings wore me out—until I learned to listen to those feelings with the safety of gentle Listening Touch.

In my grief, I didn't explore what it might be like to simply do the basics: my daily devotional time, the cooking and cleaning, bathing, making money, making love, paying bills, and caring for myself and my immediate family. What if I were excused from sending birthday cards and thank-you notes for the next year? What if I had permission to say no to committee meetings, social events, and taking care of others?

In the Jewish tradition, sitting shivah extends for seven days. It provides the time and space to just be. Life is not considered normal, and those grieving are allowed to suspend usual activities. The mourners do not work, except to clean or cook. They do not bathe, shave, change their clothes, have sex, study, learn, or wear leather shoes. They feel their feet on the floor. They and their friends sit on cushions or low stools close to the earth. They allow people to do for them. They do not return to work three days after the funeral, as most Americans must do.

In many religious traditions, life begins in the garden. We come from dust, and to dust we return. When one is sitting shivah, close to the earth, she is able to wail. It is supported, expected.

It was only once, the day after Reed's departure, that this primal emotion erupted through my body. It would be four years until the trauma and grief now living in my body would be triggered by gentle Listening Touch and released as wailing.

What I discovered from the Gift of Exhaustion:

> *Wail* your grief; keeping it in is exhausting. This means crying at the top of your lungs. Your crying is *loud*, the sounds are prolonged. You are Intentionally Mourning when you *wail*. It releases the toxins from your body. You may sound like a coyote.

> Self-care is the foundation of moving through grief. Listen to what you need. Sit down or sleep when you need to. *Stop* pushing through your fatigue.

> Realize that exhaustion is a part of Raw and Fragile Grief. Embrace it. Resisting takes energy. Imagine yourself melting like butter into your bed.

27

Take the *first 90* days *off*.

Put everything *on hold* for a *year*.

Allow the fatigue, the overwhelming roller coaster of feeling. Don't resist.

Simply do the basics.

Say *no*.

Learn gentle Listening Touch to deeply listen to yourself from a place of safety and strength.

When I notice exhaustion in my body I ask: *How am I taking care of myself in this moment?*

The Gifts from Beyond

SATURDAY, JANUARY 24–FEBRUARY 24, 2014

<figure>❧ ◈ ❧</figure>

My head hits the pillow, and I am immediately asleep. Last night at this time, I was at the hospital holding the hand of my son. Reed's face was bandaged, with only his lips visible. The ventilator tube protruding from his mouth was like some primordial tongue.

I am jolted awake, along with Edward, by what sounds like someone bumping into the dresser in Reed's room.

"What was that?" His voice is hoarse.

Bounding from bed, we are like ninjas moving past Vincent's door. I hear him roll over as I take a step closer to Reed's room. Alan is asleep on the living room couch downstairs. *What made that noise?* Edward and I look at one another in Reed's silent room. The moonlight illumines his empty bed. The leaves on the hibiscus tree close to his dresser are still. Aware of Vincent, we stifle our sobs as we embrace. Fear grips our hearts as we cautiously return to our bedroom. *Is Reed a ghost?*

The next morning as I shower, I wail, "What has happened to my son? Where is Reed? Where is his soul?"

Then, one by one, angels come into my cave of fear.

The first "God sign" is the coyote. Perhaps it is called in by my wailing, my first healthy behavior of Intentional Mourning.

Nadine Truex, a wise woman of my church, appears in my bright galley kitchen, unaware of the mortician's recent visit. The mortician had collected Reed's burial clothes, the confirmation suit that was such an important part of his life history—now a part of his obituary. I am still shaking from that transfer of my beloved son's clothing to a stranger.

"I've dusted this angel for twenty-three years, and now it is time for you to have him," she tells me, placing a small marble statue in my cupped hands. The alabaster choir boy has his eyes closed and arms folded on his choir-robed belly. His angelic wings are visible from all sides; his chin tips back as he sings from rounded lips.

I am yet unaware that this is God's loving answer to my plaintive question. I hug Nadine in gratitude, as I have so many times over the years. Then I collapse into the support of my prayer chair. I look up to see Tom Gunther once again.

He has just arrived from church and thrusts a small white box toward me. "I was asked to give these to you."

Reverend Tom hands me an envelope as well. There is a gold metallic cross stitched upon the card. The note reads:

> Dear Ed, Georgena, and Vincent,
>
> Our deepest sympathy and love to you. This angel is not new ... but when you stop to think about it, many are not. This angel always stood by Mary and Joseph and the two kissing angels that are now yours. He always was one of my favorites. Sometimes, he would tip over and land on one of the wobbly sheep, but we would always set him up again ... so that he could always be there ... make a joyful noise unto the Lord!
>
> Whenever you look at this angel, listen ... and be at Peace.
>
> Love, M.D. and Sandee Linde

Just six weeks earlier, Sandee had comforted me with tiny kissing angels after Dad's death by heart attack.

Now, I open the white box and lift out two tissue-paper bundles. The first contains a fuzzy little white sheep with a tiny sea-green bow and a golden bell around its neck. Unwrapping the second gift, I gasp. A delicate white ceramic boy angel, eyes closed, plays a reed flute. His curls are like Reed's fine blond hair was at age two. I hear God's loving answer to my questions. I say a silent prayer of thanksgiving, knowing Reed is on his way, enfolded in light.

Others, too, see signs that Reed's soul is soaring.

For Vincent, it is a Broncos win of the Super Bowl, one day after his brother is pronounced dead.

At the cemetery, I have Myrna Vincent bring hundreds of green and white helium-filled balloons, the color of Reed's soccer team. As people of all ages release them, they form a cross before disappearing into the eastern sky. Marge Winder later tells me that her gaze was riveted on one lone white balloon, drawn to the southern sky. Suddenly it was met by a brilliant ball of white light. The dazzling light appeared to lead the white one. Immediately, both vanished, leaving her heart filled with the truth that Reed was heading for heaven.

The day after Reed's funeral, winter returns to Nebraska. The sun goes under a dark sky, reflecting the condition of our hearts.

On February 24, 1998, exactly one month to the day, the phone rings at six o'clock in the evening. It is the psychiatrist's office, asking if we could come at seven because there has been a cancellation. My pleaser self says "yes" and moves into fast-forward. As I hurry to set the dining room table, the sunshine catches my eye. It has been weeks since we've seen a sunset. The dreariness that enveloped us January 24 mirrors our souls. I call to Vincent as I dash past him in our galley kitchen, "Come see the sunset." Edward bounds out behind me.

There in the western sky, we behold a spectacular sunset with wide alternating bands of denim blue and peony pink. Truly Reed is decorating heaven. This picture is exactly the width of our condominium, flanked by blue sky on the left and puffy pink clouds on the right. I need my camera to capture this gift, but the camera, like my heart, is empty.

Vincent turns to go inside. "We have to eat and get to the office. I'll finish the fajitas."

As he moves, the pink clouds drift. "Look!" I shout to Edward as I point to the signature forming before our eyes: R-e-e- and then Edward traces the big "D" aloft, exactly like the one Reed always made.

"Surely Reed's in heaven," I breathe, as relief washes over me.

31

"Yes, and God's got him signing his artwork!" Edward notes.

I begin to write the "God signs" down. Each time I do so, my faith grows deeper roots in my heart.

Eventually, there will be fertile ground to welcome and commune with Reed.

I had heard many times before Reed's departure that he was "an old soul." When he was only nine, he created two birthday cards for me with pencil drawings. Vincent's inscription read, "Happy Birthday. The older you get the better you get. We don't care— we always love you." Reed wrote, "I am so glad that I chose you for my Mother. You always listen to me."

It was an interesting inscription. Where had that thought come from?

In our *new mourning*, we become aware that our beloved communicates with us from the other side. These are called after-death communications. They take the form of electrical impulses that result in lights blinking on and off, as well as TV shows and radio songs coming on at just the moment we are thinking of our departed. Signs on billboards and license plates, pictures in the clouds, and people bringing messages with the exact words of our departed—these things have been documented over and over.

Today, I might receive an unexpected text from Vincent, who is in San Diego. In the same way, I may receive a communication from Reed using nature as a backdrop for jets, or in a sunset which I've come to trust, a message that says, "Hi, Mom."

Often, loved ones still on earth do not have the openness and perception to receive these loving communications. They are on the radio station of grief, and the frequency from beyond cannot reach the mourner. It takes trust to believe these messages, especially when the departed has been self-destructive, leaving by his own hand.

That trust was confirmed when I became able to communicate with him directly as a medium a decade later.

Mom:

Even before I pulled that trigger, my Soul called for help to the other side. I was truly in a state of emotional emergency. My Soul was calling 911. Mrs. Blinn had it precisely right in my eulogy when she said I had an emotional hijacking.

Being an Old Soul, as you have heard about me so many times, my transition to the other side was uniquely mine. It truly was a team effort to get me through because suicide was not my plan when I left the school that night. You had it right, Mom, when you figured out my killing myself was really an impulsicide. (I love how you make you words that really fit the Higher Consciousness that we all finally are experiencing.)

It was me being too hard on myself that sent me into that panic Friday night. I wouldn't be able to hang out in the locker room to encourage the guys. I, the encourager, was banished. They needed me, a peer to keep their heads up. To remind them that if they don't have confidence in themselves, how can anyone else? I completely lost confidence in myself that night. I was so ashamed.

Many believe that those of us who take our own lives are in Hell forever. I am telling you that is not the truth. There is no cut-and-dried answer for suicide because each individual suicide is uniquely different. The old paradigm of suicide was based on the belief that the particular mind or body is in complete control of what is happening all the way up to the last moment. What we are learning is that there are people like me who just "snap" as Mrs. Blinn put into words.

The current collective consciousness is impacting and shifting the way suicides are experiencing the afterlife. Because more people are aware, but not in control, in the

physical body in the waking state before that action occurs,
there is hope for every soul who transitions as suicide.

Remember what happened two weeks after Uncle
Mark died from his gunshot to his head? You were out in the
afternoon sun praying when he came walking across your
beautiful meditation meadow. He, too, was peaceful. His
face was healed and whole. He stood in his truth-telling you
to make sure that everyone knew he continued on in power,
peace and love. You went right into the house and tearfully
dictated the message for everyone in your family to hear.

- Reed

The old belief that suicides are sent to limbo is just that—an old, fear-based belief. What is a belief? A thought with an emotion wrapped around it, repeated over and over until it automatically influences our behavior.

Science is proving that we are all connected. A thought sent to another in an isolation chamber makes it through. Prayer travels across miles and is received by the one being prayed for. The energy that we are as humans is released at the time of our death and moves into another plane of existence. It is similar as to when water boils and turns to steam.

Do not despair. Their love continues for you.

A New Mourning

It is time for a new mourning—for each of us to embrace new thoughts:
We are energy, and energy is neither created nor destroyed.
The essence of our beloved lives on in another form that few of us see.
Set the intention to listen to your intuition
(your God-Self, your Essence),
Begin to notice details that you see,
Feel the senses that you experience:
You will be able to receive their messages.
Before you get out of bed each morning,
In between sleep and waking, melt like butter.
Then give yourself permission:

"I am allowing myself to receive communication from
_____."

Be the radio station that your beloved can access.

Exhale like a lion, breathe in deeply, pause,

and breathe out twice as long.

Turn your attention to your day.

Accept and appreciate the communications that you receive.

Discovering the Gift of Receiving

JANUARY 24–MARCH 1998

I was able to sleep and the cry from the time I awoke at 4 a.m. until Vincent returned home from school. He had returned to school February second. I was very grateful that I was able to attend to work with only several daily phone calls. The staff at the office contacted clients for me.

I had no energy to cook, so I gladly stepped aside as Vincent lost himself in creating delicious meals. When together, we had minutes of clarity. One evening, as we three sat at the table enjoying Vincent's super-super nachos, I turned to him. "You do not have to live for you and Reed. You are just you: Vincent."

Edward, sitting beside me, reached out and touched Vincent's shoulder. "Yes. Live your life as Vincent," he added.

Another time, as Edward and I headed out the door, Vincent handed us a picnic lunch he'd made for our road trip to Lincoln. "Thank you, Son. I appreciate this so much," said Edward. "Remember, you are not ultimately responsible for taking care of us."

"I got it, Dad. This was something I wanted to do today. It was fun for me." Vincent replied.

At the same time that we were trying to teach our only living son that he didn't have to take care of us, I had to learn to let others take care of me.

Accepting help and receiving from others came as an unbidden gift of Raw Grief.

I was raised on the "it is more blessed to give than to receive" concept. Those around me did not realize that giving and receiving are two sides of the same coin. Hearts were broken by Reed's departure. People wanted to help. The part of me that had always done for others was flattened like a reed in a gale.

Indeed, grief brings up in us those hidden parts of ourselves longing to be healed. At this point in journey, I did not know how to receive. Not knowing terrified me.

The receiving began the day of Reed's passing, January 24, 1998. The frigid night gave way to a spring-like day. People came with their disbelief. A brilliant, funny leader admired by adults as well as their children and teens, was gone. How had this happened? Many parents had been up all night with their teens trying to absorb this new reality.

They gathered in our kitchen, in the living room, upstairs in the rooms of Vincent and Reed. Some who had been at the game shared details of the night before. Several kids spoke up who had been pulled out of the bleachers and questioned. Two basketball players came forward who had witnessed Reed's final vow as he hit the locker. Their testimony confounded us all even more.

What had happened between that moment of promising to return next year and the moment he entered the garage?

By afternoon, some of the mourners simply could not stand and talk any more. They came to me where I sat cocooned in the wing-backed chair, my prayer chair, and softly asked what they could do.

Their question jolted me. We had a wake and a funeral ahead of us. Recalling Mark's, Mother's, and Dad's funerals, I began to let my driver-self delegate.

I gathered photos, sending fathers and sons to have them enlarged. Scooping up our shoes, I gratefully handed them over to be polished by others eager to serve. Moving into the laundry room, I collected wrinkled shirts for those who wanted to iron. All but Reed's.

His I would iron myself, for the last time.

My dear friend Kandace Pile and her girls saw that my fatigue was too great to walk the dog. They would just go to the back yard, unleash our beagle, Sara, and vanish for an hour. They came regularly, simply being present for Sara, and for us. I did not resist their kindness.

Friends and family took over my kitchen in those days leading up to and following Reed's funeral. The flood of food from these first responders was generous and overwhelming.

What I know now is that death creates a sense of emergency. Things are not usual. There is a vortex of swirling energy that envelops and affects those touched by this loss, in varying degrees. We have seen it countless times as strangers and neighbors, when family and friends are magnetized by need.

We welcomed the loving support, overwhelmed. As the days went on, I began wishing that instead of the flood of food early on, some of the supporters had brought gift cards for later use. On those days and nights, standing in the kitchen was a Herculean task. Getting out of the house, away from the vortex of grief, was a necessity. Even take-out would have been a godsend. But sitting in a restaurant was difficult. We would have to engage with others. So I came home to the work of having to prepare the next meal.

Days after Reed's funeral came the test of graciously receiving from others. Could I step into a new pattern of allowing others to give to me?

My friend Kris dropped by one morning, two weeks after Reed's funeral. When I heard the doorbell, I knew I had a choice. I could either open the door, revealing what a mess I was, or not respond. More than any other time in my life, I needed courage.

Still in my bathrobe, with my tear-stained face and my bone-weariness, I opened the door. "Please come in, Kris." I welcomed her, that late morning hour.

"I just had to see you," she said. "To hug you. To know that somehow you are still in one piece."

Kris began to cry. Her embrace warmed me, bringing me back to life. For a moment, I could feel my body, and this contact with another human being pulled me away from grief's grip, creating safety. For a moment, the numbness of raw grief vanished in my body.

"I am still here," I said, feeling my smile rekindle so brightly it could have lit up the room. We sat together, two soccer moms, grateful for this heart-to-heart time.

Opening the door had been the right choice.

School officials did not come. Instead, they delegated Reed's guidance counselor, who came to deliver the contents of his locker. I had no warning of her arrival, but since it was late afternoon, I was dressed.

"Please come in, Mrs. Neal," I said, the ever-welcoming hostess.

"No, thank you. I won't be long. Here are the things from Reed's locker. There are several art projects that his art teacher will bring by." She remained in the entryway. She stood in the exact place where I had said good-bye to Reed just ten days before.

"Many students have been by," I reported. "How do you think they are doing?" Words such as "trauma," "grief," and "mourning" had rarely entered my vocabulary up to this point in my life.

"Well," she began, folding her thin arms around the notebook and bag she carried. "We were really worried that the full-page eulogy, the picture of Reed, and your thank-you in the newspaper would send some over the edge." She voiced the concern I had seen on the faces of the officials that night in the emergency room.

My body tightened. Obviously Reed's death had unleashed a ferocious fear among the administrators of the Norfolk High School Panthers.

"We chose to pay the newspaper for that," I responded. "So many people were comforted by the insights expressed by Diane. We had hundreds of requests for copies of her eloquent eulogy, so it felt like something easy to do." I was scrambling to try to explain, to try to create common ground.

Why did I suddenly feel like a victim—like I had done wrong by publicly expressing my gratitude? We'd placed the ad at huge personal financial cost. We had simply attempted to meet the needs of the parents who wanted the firm foundation Diane had provided as the educator she was. The kids were obviously grasping for one last look at Reed since his casket was closed. Now they had a picture to hold on to.

The photograph in the ad was taken the day Reed found the almond in his Epiphany cake. It truly captured his humility, as well as my heart. Once again, he'd been the winner. Finding that almond was supposed to bring him extraordinary luck in 1998.

I swallowed hard at the thought.

The guidance counselor said nothing as she handed me the notebook and bag.

"Thank you for coming," I finished, standing straight and tall as I could. "Please know that it is our intention to get these kids safely through their grief." I smiled, knowing I was speaking the truth.

She nodded and faintly smiled as she turned her back to depart. I did not know if she was a mother of sons.

During that time, we received three letters from teens who shared the powerful impact of Reed's life.

One student wrote:

> *I started making wrong choices in school with friends. I was feeling a lot of pressure because of sports and to just be the person everyone assumed I was. One night, some things happened, and my parents forbade me to see the boy I had spent almost every day with for a long time. Everything had been leading up to this, and I decided I wanted it all to stop. Then I heard about Reed. This showed me that people care and will help if I only ask. What you wrote in the paper really meant a lot to me: "No burden is too heavy that can't be lifted by talking to someone." In a sense, Reed saved my life. I just wanted to thank you from the bottom of my heart.*

Gladys showed up one morning with hot soup. Habitually gracious, I invited her to come and sit. She simply said, "I think of you so often and wanted this to warm you."

Not only was I courageous to open the door in those days and months after the funeral, but so were those who came.

My friend Sherry came every Sunday afternoon for months. She was the mom of middle-schoolers, with busy, short weekends. Yet we'd go up to my bedroom in the four o'clock sun, and she would recount stories she'd heard about Reed that week. Sherry served as a speech-language pathologist in the public schools and was among teachers and students who had been touched by Reed's ability to see the needs of another. She told about Reed just sitting with a frustrated boy in math class. In his own gifted way, Reed had unraveled the problem. I never knew all the things my son had done to uplift others.

When I asked about his day, Reed's answers had always been brief. He had lived in the moment and planned for the future. How comforting to read his eighth-grade journal entry about me to Sherry! "My mom always has time," he wrote, "to talk or do something fun with me no matter what she's got going. A hundred times out of a hundred when she picks me up after school, she asks me how my day went I usually just say, 'It was okay' or 'fine.' But about one out of a hundred times she asks me how my day was and I've got something I really want to tell her, she'll listen to me. That's what I'm thankful for concerning my mom, is that she'll always listen to me no matter what."

Having Sherry as a witness and companion through grief's grip gave me space. Psychological air. It was the very thing Reed had not been given that night.

Now, I took it in. I rested in the moment and asked for countless details. The movies played in my mind of my son's kindness; they projected onto the screen of my heart. I was learning to receive easily because I was desperate for what was being given. I was assured that the violence Reed had done to himself was not the essence of who Reed was.

Sherry would receive my deepest gratitude for those afternoons in the years to come.

Reed's death brought me to my knees. I needed help. People often asked "What can I do?" and I replied, "Just put yourself in my shoes." It was helpful when they thought about what it took to keep a household going. Clothes needed to be washed and ironed. Clean underwear was a must. Junk mail needed to be shredded. Cars needed washing and gas. Plants need to be watered and talked to. Yards needed to be cared for.

Chris Walker French-braided my hair and did my nails for Reed's funeral. She wanted to do more. We had gotten hundreds and hundreds of cards. So I asked her to organize them for me. Some were so comforting that I wanted to be able to easily retrieve them. She bought several large containers and set about the task of alphabetizing and filing them. What a gift!

We moved those cards from Nebraska to Colorado to Oregon in four short years. People had poured their hearts into them. I gladly received these offerings of love, even though most brought me to tears.

I came to discover that when we give, we are in control. When we receive, we are in acceptance and trust. The offerings of food, help, communication, and memorials to Reed brought us closer, the givers and receivers.

There was a bond that formed with the elderly woman who brought angel food cake the day of Reed's wake. After reading his obituary, she was moved to reach out to total strangers. The love on her face as she delivered it enfolded me once again in that Powerful Presence of Friday night.

I did not need the cake. It was the depth of her love I received.

Discovering the Gift of Receiving, I learned to:

> Choose to let others take care of me.
> Accept others' help and receive from them.
> Delegate.
> Consider requesting restaurant gift cards when people asked to help.
> Allow another to accompany me through grief's grip as my listening witness.

Discovering a Pattern: Repeat or Delete?

MARCH 1998

Friends and family lavished us with love. Checks poured in for a life-sized bronze statue of Reed to be created by Art Anderson, a local sculptor Edward had engaged. The sculpture would depict Reed playing soccer with all of his natural fluidity, one arm cocked arm back and one foot directing the ball.

A natural athlete, Reed had been known for expert zigs and zags, an intuition for precise positioning, and speed that earned him the nickname, "Speedy Reedy" as a child. Vincent would serve as a model for the project, which would ultimately be a gift to soccer players across Nebraska that would come to rest in Tranquility Park Youth Soccer field in Omaha.

There were hundreds of thank-you notes to write. I immediately answered the letters from the three teens who had decided against suicide. I affirmed their lives. Just like Reed, it was natural for me to inspire others. I wanted to cheer them on in their choice to live.

As I took pen in hand to write another letter, I was pulled away by my thoughts. *I'd chosen to give Reed space. Why hadn't I taken his hand? Why had I walked away? I had abandoned my son.* I was overcome with guilt by my actions.

Each time the final scene played of our last moment together, I was engulfed by grief. Edward and I continued to weep for days on end, although it had been two months.

I dried my eyes and returned to my list of generous, caring people to thank.

My mother had always insisted I write a thank-you note for any gift within the first week after it was received. This was what played in the back of my mind and spurred me onward to keep the practice.

Thinking of Mother, I realized I was not the only one who had lost a son.

She, too, had felt the sting of a son's suicide and directed the blame at herself. Yet my brother Mark's sudden death in June 1994 had not been her doing. It had stemmed from his paranoid schizophrenia.

Mark was a gifted, kind, creative, sensitive, generous man. In high school, he was a distance track star, an offensive guard on the football team, a stellar student and leader. But he was literally on the run. He began drinking in high school to ramp down from his fast-paced schedule. And then alcohol became his addiction.

In college, Mark and our brother, Alan, shared the fraternity, Phi Tau. Alan's idea of a party included downing a six-pack of Budweiser. Mark's idea was to drink half a bottle of Wild Turkey. The difference in toxicity to their brains was immense.

In every area of his life, Mark held impossibly high standards. He emulated Mother's perfectionism. An obsession with being perfect had become our family trait.

One summer, Alan and Mark nearly came to blows. It was toward the end of a scorching afternoon, and they both worked on a roofing crew. By five o'clock, Alan was whipped and ready to go. He was picking up his tools when Mark insisted they stay until a particular task was finished. Alan was furious. "Why do you always insist on everything being done perfectly?" he growled.

"You know what Mom always says—whatever is worth doing is worth doing right," Mark said as he turned back to the task at hand.

Alan's anger dissipated instantly. It was no use arguing with this family value. It took their last ounce of energy, but they stayed and did the work. This was Mark's approach to life: give it everything you've got, and then some.

Another example of Mark's going the extra mile happened during the last few months of his life, as he was making his daily commute from

Hastings to Grand Island. He spotted a young man thumbing a ride in the Nebraska rain. Mark pulled to the highway shoulder. "Where you headed?"

"Up to the Interstate and then on to Lincoln," was the man's reply. Mark not only took the man to Interstate 80, but drove him the hundred miles to Lincoln, Nebraska, and gave him his sack lunch. Mark was late that day for his job as a registered financial representative of a national firm. It was his choice. He made up for it by simply staying late at the office. He knew that taking time for this young man in need was important. It would show the man that someone cared.

One Sunday morning while attending church, Mark heard the minister say, "Anyone who takes medication just does not have enough faith in Jesus." These words would have a fatal impact upon him.

Mother and Dad heard those words, too, when Mark came over on a Monday night. Both saw Mark's faraway look, his increased anxiety and restlessness. They both urged Mark to begin taking his medication once again so he would not relapse and require hospitalization. Their loving parental care and urging resulted in Mark storming out of the house. Their last encounter with their beloved son was an argument.

Mark did get his prescription filled on that Tuesday. That evening, though, the medication had not yet taken effect. When he went to pick up his three children for his night with them, his former wife looked at him closely. "No," she said, folding her arms in the doorway, acting on her responsibility to protect her children. "I can see it in your eyes. You're not taking your medication, and I won't let you take the kids."

Mark returned to his home, watched DVDs of his children, and wrote a note saying how weary he was of his disease. Then he kissed the barrel of a shotgun good-night. Mark was thirty-nine.

Mother's sense of guilt tormented her after Mark's death. The *Omaha World Herald* printed an article on the high incidence of paranoid schizophrenia. It drew a connection between the polio virus, resulting in high fevers in pregnant mothers, and an increased incidence of this mental illness.

As it happened, Mother was a night nurse at the time she was pregnant with Mark and, unfortunately, she contracted polio. She was in an iron lung for weeks. I remember my five-year-old-self feeling so helpless when

Dad took us to the hospital to "visit." Our visit consisted of staring down at Mother from the garden-level window outside the hospital. She seemed so far away. We all smiled bravely at one another.

Mother chided herself for not adhering to medical precautions. Thankfully, Dad had chosen not to have my gifted, sensitive brother aborted after being asked by the doctor to make this decision alone. Perhaps this bond between them, even before Mark was born, made Mark Dad's favorite. Even so, the end of Mark's life had come far too soon, by his own doing.

Mother's guilt and regret, from her first worry as a pregnant mom, to her anguish over his suicide, had all become a burden that was too much for her to bear.

I thought about all this now as I sat at the table with my pen and stationery. I glanced up at the chandelier, the light dimming through my tear-weary eyes.

A slender cobweb appeared. Not large and intricate—only a single strand. My mind jolted through time, taken back by the cobweb. It was September, two years after Mark's death, and we were all trying to carry on as best as we could in our state of Fragile Grief. Mother had invited me to her home for a luncheon for her nieces.

I had delegated my patients to my colleagues and eagerly made the several-hour drive to Hastings for this special occasion. Arriving early, I noticed a dusty white strand hanging left to right from the burgundy blinds in Mother's guest bathroom.

I felt a tightness in my throat and gasped out loud. I had never seen a cobweb in my mother's house.

Instantly, I knew something was wrong. The truth was, for years I had been observing and analyzing the behavior of patients, looking for cognitive deficits. When I noticed memory deficits, lack of insight, problem-solving issues, or disorganization, I would support those patients with strategies that would help them return to normal function. But in that moment, I made the choice to put aside my profession for the day. I removed the cobweb with a guest towel, wiped the sink, and decided to let it go. I would leave my Sherlock Holmes hat in the bathroom and enjoy being my mother's daughter.

Several weeks later, a CT scan of her brain revealed a glioblastoma in the right parietal lobe of her brain. No wonder she had not seen that cobweb on the left! Dad then also had an answer for why she had nearly driven into the left side of the garage door when parking the car. She had a left visual field cut and was simply not seeing images on the left unless she turned her head to compensate.

Mother had surgery, radiation, seizures, and rehab—and then died in July 1997.

When someone asked her, "Why did you get cancer, Betty?" her reply was simply, "Why not?" never, "Poor me." She was not a victim.

My mother was one of the most responsible people I have ever met. When she decided to undertake a task, it was *done*. Mother had an eye for detail that added confidence, as she loved to do things her way. She was the consummate project manager long before I ever knew there was such a career field.

No wonder Reed had the follow-through that could move a mountain.

It was a morning in May 1997. We were in Mother's bedroom. She was sitting in her wheelchair. Dad had done her makeup, and, even though pain shone through her eyes, she was beautiful. She looked at me and smiled. "You know, Georgena, I wish I had not been so particular about the house. I could have spent more time playing with you kids and less time cleaning." She meant every word.

I squeezed her hand. "Oh, but I remember you playing fox and geese with us out in the snow," I told her. "Also, you'd join us in checkers. And what fun we had making popcorn balls for Halloween! You always got the orange color so perfect." My heart was light, and the words came easily. I felt blessed to have so many wonderful memories.

"Oh, I couldn't have asked for a better daughter," she said and we hugged each other tightly, weeping.

So many memories of love, loss, and understanding flooded me as I sat at the oak table writing letters and grieving. Still in Raw Grief, my mind was confused.

What I needed was a greater understanding of the mind-body connection. I had not even heard of such a thing until a couple of years earlier when I'd read *You Can Heal Your Life* by Louise Hay.

There was a line in the book that had felt like a kick to my gut. Hay explained that the probable cause of cancer was "a deep secret or grief eating away at the self." She'd also written that the probable cause for a brain tumor was "Incorrect computerized beliefs. Stubborn. Refusing to give up old patterns."

But in this moment, nearly two months after Reed's death, I collapsed into a puddle, supported by the table.

My mother had loved me. And she had given me a priceless gift. I realized I had a choice as to whether I would be eaten by guilt at my memory of Reed's last hour.

Such had been the case every time the image flashed in my mind of not taking Reed's hand.

Instead of guilt, I could recognize my pattern. I had created a pattern that said, "I will handle this myself."

In eight short months, I would begin a training that would completely transform how I dealt with guilt and grief. In fact, it would change my life and the life of every client I touched with my hands as a Synergist.

But I knew nothing of this right now. I faced a choice. *Would I allow these negative thoughts to keep me stuck?* I began in that very moment to focus on the power of my choice.

My focus was fleeting. Over and over, I had to remind myself that I had this power of choice. I would shift out of guilty thoughts causing me pain. I would find myself slipping back. I felt like a bobblehead. One minute, I was aware of the destructive power of these thoughts and the next, I was drowning in them.

It was also at this point that I realized Vincent needed a mother. Like Reed, he had grieved deeply for his Grandma Betty, Granddad George, and Uncle Mark. Each had died too young. And now, Vincent grieved a brother, too. I was not going to continue with these potentially harmful, guilty thoughts but would make the most of the life we had. So I bobbled on. Over and over, I spun the story around, coming to my senses.

I began to follow, intuitively, a model of grief that had yet to emerge in my future:

- Recognize the grief and what thought triggered it.
- Release the grief with tears and other available tools.
- Replace the grief with a new focus. Soon that focus would be the training in the Rubenfeld Synergy Method® that I would begin November 1, my mother's birthday.

As I discovered the old pattern of guilty thoughts and the resulting behavior, I:

- Recognized that I had the freedom of choice.
- Repeatedly released the guilt with the awareness of my intentions.
- Replaced the guilt-triggering thoughts with my awareness that each of us is is responsible for our life.

The Gift of Putting Why to Rest

MARCH 1998

Sudden death cuts the flow of life as we know it. The car accident, stroke, heart attack, or most confounding of all, suicide—we do not usually get to say good-bye. We wonder; "What if?" and "Why?" can color our world forever if we allow it.

Vincent, Edward, and I had been fortunate to see my dad on December 4, 1997, the day before he dropped dead of a heart attack. We were not supposed to, but we decided on Wednesday to provide the cookies for a Friday afternoon Christmas tea in one of our local nursing homes. Dad could bring the cookies from our favorite bakery in Hastings and meet us in Omaha on Thursday, in the late afternoon. He was flying out the next morning to return home to Pennsylvania for his sixtieth class reunion.

"Hi, Dad, would you be willing to be a cookie guy?" My driver-self had learned to be straight to the point when communicating with my dad.

"Sure, honey, what do you need?" he sounded the happiest I'd heard him since Mother's departure just four-and-a-half months earlier.

"Oh, eight dozen cookies from Eileen's for a Christmas tea here on Friday afternoon. We will meet you with a check at your airport motel. Just name the time."

"Will the boys be with you? I want to give Vincent a huge hug on his appointment to the Merchant Marine Academy. I am so proud of him. Reed's been on my mind, and I want to see him, too."

"Well, Vincent will be with us, but Reed will not because he has basketball practice. Got your pencil ready for the order?"

When we met the next day, I was amazed to see my dad bubbling with plans for the next phase of his life. He had grieved by sitting in front of Mother's picture in their bedroom. He'd talk to her, weep, and tell her how much he loved and missed her. Dad was demonstrative, so crying at weddings and funerals was natural for him. My aunt had noted, "Your dad seems more in love with your Mother now than ever before."

He had told me at Thanksgiving that he'd be done with his intense grieving on December 1. When I saw him that day, he was definitely moving on. I was thrilled for him.

So when the call came late the next night, I could not believe the words.

It was Aunt Mary. "Georgena, your dad sat down on the couch after dinner and died."

My brain and my heart quickly imagined my parents together once again. As with Mark's departure, my sadness quickly passed.

Reed, however, held his grief in. He was frustrated by Mark's sudden death. Often, as we left church, I would see Reed's face turn ashen. At first I would ask, "Are you thinking about Uncle Mark?" and his eyes would fill with tears as he turned his back to me. I learned to simply put my arm around his waist and say nothing, thankful he let me do this. I did not know how deadly this held-in grief could be.

Reed had also missed saying good-bye to both his Grandma Betty and his Granddad George. With Dad's blessing, Reed had written a story about his grandma to be read at her funeral. He had boarded a bus for a high-level soccer camp in Iowa the morning she departed. We all thought it was the best choice for Reed. Looking back, I know that it was not. He missed out on being with all of us, experiencing the energy of his family, and feeling his grief while he mourned with us.

The scene of Reed weeping alone at the foot of my dad's casket on a bitter December day still brings me to tears. He was not willing to be comforted as he mourned deeply, privately holding up his hand to stop me, telling me to stay away.

The tragedy of suicide gives rise to the ponderings of every detail known and unknown. *What didn't I see? What could I have done differently? Why did this happen?*

I had invited people to tell me their answer to "Why?" There were fourteen unique answers. Some felt cruel, like the woman who stated that Reed was headed to the life of an alcoholic, so he died to set us free.

Another answer was simply stupid. One father implied that, had I child-proofed my home, this would not have happened. He told the story of how he had taught his own son what a shotgun could do by blowing a watermelon to bits. I informed him that Reed had earned his hunter safety card just the year before. I graciously accepted the book he brought me and then ushered him to the door.

It was the realization that "Reed had never failed publicly" that hit me in the gut. Of course he had never done so. Not until this time. Life is a "do it to yourself project" as Denis Waitley says. And he'd reached a point in the project where he didn't know how to cope.

Reed taught me that, being too hard on yourself can kill ya.

His was really not suicide. His death was impulse-icide. His journals would reveal that he had planned to letter in five sports in four years. He knew he was here to make a difference.

My parents had seen his drive, his perfectionism, and his determination to make a difference. He reminded them of Mark.

When they talked with me, I could feel their fear. In response, I went to see a woman in Omaha who practiced Neuro-Linguistic Programming (NLP). I did not want to project any fear onto Reed. At the end of the session, the woman had me walk a timeline, envisioning Reed at the end of it. I could only see him at age thirty. I would later learn that some say this is the age we return to on the other side.

What I did not do was interrupt Reed's self-criticism. I did not know how to do that myself.

What is a reed? It is a slender stalk of grass fashioned from a series of hollow, interconnecting chambers. The secret to its strength is its many joints. They give it the flexibility to bend until it is almost flattened and then rise again, in a wind strong enough to fell trees. Paradoxically, but almost

predictably, those same joints are also its vulnerable point. If force is not spread over the whole reed, but is focused intensely on a single point of joining, the reed snaps apart with unexpected ease.

—Diane Marie Blinn

Reed was the star with huge gifts and talents. He was to put Norfolk on the map again, like Johnny Carson.

Then a switch went off.

A supernova illustrates the most violent death of a star we know. It occurs when there is a massive energy build-up, which means something has to give. The core of the star turns to iron. This dense core collapses, crushing atoms, time, and space. Finally, this giant star explodes, blowing itself to pieces. The super-powerful explosion of nuclear energy becomes a black hole.

The shame in Reed had begun to build. Like the iron core in a supernova, it got heavier and heavier. He condemned himself, no doubt. I know because I have done it to myself. I exaggerate in my mind what I have done.

My own iron core told me that not taking Reed's hand was an unforgiveable error. Like Reed, I would take the blame for what I had done.

Like Reed, I wanted to shrink and hide, knowing I could have made other choices.

In Reed's case, weighed down by self-loathing, he finally snapped.

He saw there was no way out of this pain except to run home where he had always been safe. With each stride, the guilt grew. Years later, I read the words of David Hawkins: "Guilt provokes rage, and killing is frequently its expression."

There was no room in his mind for self-compassion. No mercy could be shown to himself. His rage flipped the switch, and my beloved son was gone. I had my *Why?*

Now I ponder: *What if suicide is the powerful catalyst for self-love?* I did not know as a mother then that there is a continuum with self-love. Ultimate self-love lies on the far right, moving left to self-compassion, to self-acceptance, to self-kindness, to self-care, to self-loathing, and finally to self-hatred and then self-destruction on the other end. How many times had I teetered in the place of self-loathing? Instead of being still and letting go of condemning thoughts, I argued with them. My mind would spin like a top.

There is a pattern to the personalities that leave by suicide. Intense, driven, serious, fun-loving to the max, pushing the envelope, impulsive, bigger-than-life—these are words that grieving mothers of sons have used to tell me of their beloved, now-departed children. How many of these young men were out of their minds with rage and self-hatred when they killed themselves? We cannot love them enough when they will not give love to themselves.

Still in my Raw Grief, my brain was not clear. I was exhausted and overwhelmed. It had not been ninety days, and I was still crying for hours, tormented by my longing for Reed's physical presence, walking in dark sadness.

How I learned to let *Why* be:

- Rest in forgiving and then loving myself a little each day.
- I began with asking Reed to forgive me for not taking his hand.
- Like my dad talking to Mother, I talked to Reed's photo while sitting in the support of my prayer chair.

Discovering the Gift of Object Permanence

April 6, 1998

One fear I had was that Reed would be forgotten—perhaps even by me. Fortunately, the act of journaling taught me that I could cherish all the memories, miracles, and gifts. We saw a psychiatrist for a few visits (until it became clear that we were counseling *him* because he was so distraught over Reed's death). One helpful admonishment was, "Keep a journal of your dreams." In a beautiful synchronicity, our friends the Searses, along with the Scheers, had already gifted us with beautiful pens and journals where we could pour out our hearts. My letters of yearning were to Spirit or Reed.

Then, about 4 a.m. the Monday after Palm Sunday, the beginning of Holy Week, I dreamed a dream that brought me back to wholeness.

In the dream, I was walking into Hastings Junior High, where I'd attended classes thirty-three years before. I was accompanied by Mother and Lisa Barnes, a woman in our business family. Larry Doerr, the minister who had married us twenty-five years earlier, officiated. Worship in this public place was in a wide hallway area defined by couches arranged in a U-shape.

Mother and I sat down with Lisa between us. As Mother leaned toward me to speak, I shot her "the look," letting her know we should set a good example for Lisa and not whisper in church.

We all stood for the "Passing of the Peace" and reached out to one another with a handshake and the phrase, "Peace be with you." When the ritual was complete, there was no room for me on the couch. I spotted the only vacant place and strode over, turning to the person on my left who occupied the end spot.

It was Reed!

I smiled, overjoyed. Reed looked at me calmly. I lassoed him with my arms, embraced him, and immediately awoke feeling his presence.

It was unmistakably an after-death communication, the third I'd received from Reed. Relief flooded my heart.

The clock read 4:30 a.m. Edward and Sara, the beagle, were snoring soundly until my bodily jolt awakened them. I was reeling from the dream. Looking up, I was even more startled.

"What do you see on the ceiling, Honey?" I asked Edward.

"Two white lights," he immediately replied, looking at the fuzzy white golf ball spots to his upper left. *What were these other-worldly light globes doing on our ceiling?* It was as if Mother and Reed had formed from the dream into two circles of light.

"Where are they coming from? Open the blinds," I instructed. "Maybe it is the street light."

Edward crept to the window, raising the fabric blinds. We gazed back at the ceiling. The circles of light remained unchanged.

He lowered the shade and returned to bed. We stared with silent intensity. The circles of light grew dimmer, faded completely, and then reappeared for another minute. Both the size of silver dollars, the one on the right had a tail like a comet. Suddenly they moved toward the window and vanished.

My heart flooded with hope. I turned to the bedside table and grabbed my journal to record the dream.

Suddenly, I realized that I had cut my mother off, silencing her with my determination to be polite in front of Lisa. I had not heard her heavenly message. This was the one and only time Mother and I had communicated in visible form with her on the other side.

Now I wondered: *When will I delete this pattern of politeness?* It persisted even in my subconscious. I let the frustration go. I focused on the dream.

Reed's peaceful presence was still palpable as I described his face, so serene, so whole. There was a power that exuded from him.

Later that morning, I sat down for another batch of thank-you notes, and I remembered a lesson I'd received in child development. I'd studied Piaget's concept of object permanence. The idea is that between birth and age two, a child realizes that things continue to exist even when they are no longer present to the senses. The ball that rolls behind the couch is still there. Mother moving into the next room and out of sight is still present.

This knowing then enhances the feeling of safety and security in the child's nervous system. Now I see it as the validation that we are all one. There really is no separation. Science has shown that we are all made from the same stardust created at the moment of the Big Bang.

This remembrance of object permanence is a concept that I had not read in any grief books, although I was reading nearly one per week as a way out of the vortex of grief.

The concept of object permanence proved to be a significant part of my grieving process.

I became aware of my longing for Reed's return. Knowing in my heart that he would never be physically present again, I began to notice that longing, like guilt, put me into the depths of despair. I began to consciously choose to remember that Reed's soul was soaring and it was I who required the attention I was giving his memory. He would only be forgotten if no one ever said his name. His friends would not let that happen.

After a time, I could declare:

In this moment, I realize that I am the child and Reed is the mother that has moved into the other room. He is merely out of my sight. The appearance of the coyote, signed sunset Reed's presence in the dream, and the orbs of light have been his after-death communications.

I realize that Reed continues to exist when he is no longer in physical form. I acknowledge that Reed can be present to me now, if only I have eyes to see clearly and a heart-mind that believes.

Discovering The Gift of Feeling Overwhelmed: Persist? Or Recognize and Relax?

FALL 1997

It was a clear, brisk morning in October. I had dropped Reed off in front of the junior high. He was happy, and we had chatted easily on the drive about his upcoming day. We'd said our "I love you"s, and the last thing I remember was his miraculous smile, the one that inevitably amped up my heart-happiness with a bright *Ta Dah!*

No sooner had I set the planner down on my desk when the phone rang. It was the junior high principal, Lee, calling to say Reed had been in a fight. "But he was so happy when he got out of the car," I said.

Thankfully, Edward was already on his way.

I would learn shortly after noon what happened as Reed collapsed into my arms with a tearful, "I am sorry, Mom. I am so sorry."

Part of Reed's initiation as a starting freshman on the cross country team was to have his head shaved by the upper classmen. The previous day had been his first appearance with this drastic one-of-a-kind look in the junior high. He had sported his bald head with a mix of pride and embarrassment.

After he had shut the car door and walked away from me, halfway up the sidewalk, he was assaulted by the word, "Skinhead!" A skateboard slammed into the back of his skull.

He knew that fighting back against his attacker meant suspension from school. He made a conscious choice not to do so. He pulled his T-shirt up over his head and kept walking toward the door of the cafeteria. The security guard watched as Reed ascended the steps, the skateboarder shouting behind him.

Reed's friend Zak came around the corner. The skateboarder lunged toward Zak. In that moment, Reed lost all self-control.

Reed slammed his fist into the face of his attacker, defending his friend.

Now, Edward stood by Reed with support. He called our attorney to prepare to press charges against the student attacker. Edward then took Reed to the police station, where he gave his statement to the police.

Yet we never filed those charges. Being understanding and forgiving was just who we were as a family.

As it turned out, Reed was suspended for three days and placed on probation for three months. Each week, we drove him to diversion activities completed with his probation officer.

I held my son that October afternoon as he wept over the news of his suspension. I fixed my eyes on his. "Reed you were attacked. You did not start this. I am so sorry this happened and that you made the choice to fight. I love you." That time he heard me and felt my supportive presence.

The phone had rung day and night for the next three days. All parents fumed that Reed was suspended, and a few even said the skateboarders just wanted a place to enjoy their sport.

Questioning the school rules, with two of our friends on the school board, Edward had long discussions with the differing groups.

It was a lesson in fighting. We fight to resist the fear of powerlessness. We fight to "fix" what we see is not right. We freeze to shut down the fear of powerlessness.

Indeed, the rabbit in winter white that sits frozen, statue-still, later hops around to release all the tension when the fox is gone.

We may flee to numb our fear of powerlessness—to run away and hide, to self-soothe with TV, food, video games, shopping, or alcohol. These are our unhealthy attempts to slow down.

Addicts numb. We, in the United States, are a nation of addicts. We are addicted not only to drugs and alcohol, work, and shopping, but to busyness, over-achieving, sports, goal-setting, and getting. The book

Speed: Facing Our Addiction to Fast and Faster and Overcoming Our Fear of Slowing Down is all about the phenomenon of addiction to doing. We believe we can do it all if we just work harder, move faster, and stay up later.

We have bought into the belief that we, through our own power, can do it all, have it all.

I was a forty-seven-year-old dynamo. Like my son, Reed, I was tightly wound. Both of us harnessed an unusual sense of urgency. We were driven to bring our talents to light, to serve others, to fill the hours of our days with the activities we valued. At times, this drive was a gift, and at other times, we simply wore ourselves out.

Reed's notebooks spelled out that timeline for lettering in five sports. The cross-country letter was achieved in the fall of his freshman year, and the soccer letter was to be awarded in the spring.

Yet despite our achievements, both Reed and I bought into the cultural expectations of success in the nineties. We believed that to achieve was to relieve the fear of unworthiness. Although we loved others and wanted to make a difference, we did not love ourselves.

Our heads rode our bodies the way a jockey drives a racehorse. We whipped ourselves into doing more and better, even when exhausted. After his burial, I would read in Reed's eighth-grade journal entry from January 31, 1997:

> *"Basketball, school, family & friends—things have been really hectic lately with all I'm trying to juggle. All of those I named (basketball, school, family & friends) play an important role in my life whether keeping in shape or becoming the person I want to be. So I don't always get enough time or the time I need to do the best in whatever it is I'm doing but I'm trying and trying to do my best to please everyone, including myself. It's hard to please everybody when there's only 24 hours in a day, but I think it's possible. I just need to find out a way how.*
>
> *P.S. My grades and class work haven't been as good as I like or as good as should be expected of me, but it is a tight*

schedule, so I'm sorry for the drop in my work, but I'll get it back up!"

A year later, Reed was dead.

I spent far too many years modeling this belief and behavior style. My sons rarely saw me simply sit and read a book, watch the clouds, or spend time in meditation and prayer. It was the same with my mother and me.

It was not until midway through Mother's illness that I came to realize how balanced her life really was—behind the scenes. I did not see her morning devotional time because she was always up before I was. Breakfast was our first daily encounter: hot food served in a safe, sparkling kitchen. Her day then moved on to her list, which seemed endless. She worked the entire day, either inside the house or as a registered nurse. She did not stay with us at the swimming pool where other mothers lounged with their drinks, chatting, their presence seeming to me like a gift. In the evening when her kitchen was sparkling again, she sat down and began her self-care out of my sight, when she would read or watch TV with my dad.

What I witnessed was my mother working from morning to night; that was what good people did.

She repeatedly admonished me to "slow down," and I was never able to reconcile her actions with her words. I would have liked to have a "practice what you preach" conversation, but we never did because I did not have the awareness that it was necessary.

What I did have was a sense of being called to greatness. It was a pattern in our family. Overachieving was the norm. We called it the Kuzma curse.

At age sixteen, Dad worked with the officials of Wilkes Barre, Pennsylvania, to create an ice rink that would benefit his entire community. He served on General McArthur's staff as an army captain. After the Americans took Tokyo, Dad spearheaded a campaign to collect food, clothes, and bandages for lepers in a colony outside the city. Like Mother, he had the heart of a helper.

Making a difference was in our bones. We could have made a difference in love and relaxation, but rather, we strove relentlessly toward our goals. Commitment, persistence, and consistency kept us moving forward until the outcome was achieved.

I moved through life with my nervous system tightly wound. I lived in a constant state of hyper-vigilance and stress. I did not feel safe. Reed and I, in our intensity, had no awareness of the harm we were doing to ourselves. We thought it was normal.

We drove ourselves, lost sleep, and feared that we were not doing enough or being enough. We struggled to manage the gifts, talents, and ideas moving constantly through our minds.

I did not model self-care for my sons because I did not even hear the term until after Reed's death. Unless we were playing or chatting in the car, Reed did not experience a relaxed mother.

Beyond Reed's driven nature, other forces came into play. Over time, I came to believe that Reed did experience an "emotional hijacking." This was the term Diane Marie Blinn brought to light in her eulogy of Reed:

*"When our sense of emergency becomes unexpectedly heightened and our adrenaline starts pumping, sensory data may pour directly through the limbic or emotional system into the control mechanisms for physical reaction, short-circuiting the usual route through the cortex, our slower but higher-order thinking center. In the immediacy of this primitive state, perhaps he was unable to see that the door he sought, out of pain, could not be directly accessed. Instead it was a second set of double doors, the first confusingly pointing **to** and only then **through** the pain. And lacking that understanding, he chose an emergency exit. As a result, in this life, we have lost our friend, our brother, our child, Reed Eggleston."*

The event was also a response to shame. Reed was lashed by shame, and he fled to the safety of home.

He was suspended from school and the basketball team. His sense of self was decimated. Everyone would know that he alone was responsible for his actions.

He felt worthless. In that moment, his brain wasn't rational enough to take in the fact that we all make mistakes.

Brene Brown explains this shame trigger in the *Power of Vulnerability*. Reed's limbic, feeling brain was overwhelmed.

Without the presence of his parents, and under the influence of alcohol, Reed collapsed onto the barrel of his granddad's shotgun.

Discovering the Gift of Recognition and Relaxation, I would learn to ask myself:

- Where do I recognize the feeling of being overwhelmed in my body?
- Do I fight, flee, or freeze?
- How do I release the sensation?

My options included breathing, sleep, healthy eating, exercise, and my spiritual practice.

PART II

Discovering the Gifts of Fragile Grief

Discovering The Gift of Body-Mind Wisdom: Ignore or Connect?

JULY 28 AND NOVEMBER 3, 1998

I arrived at Reed's grave late in the morning on July 28. The marble slab cradled a work of art. Above Reed's artistic signature flew the pair of mallard ducks he had created to win the Nebraska Duck Stamp. Gracing each side were reeds, one bent in half.

It was hot that morning but not hot enough to melt the blue candle wax that had soaked into Reed's headstone, porous and easy to mar.

The night before, we'd had a backyard barbeque with all of Reed's favorite foods. Teens chomped on yellow ears of corn and mouth-watering ribs. We celebrated Reed's sixteenth birthday with hilarious stories.

Everyone had gone up to his room one last time to take an article of clothing, a piece of art, or some other treasure. The room would soon be redecorated and turned into Edward's office.

Later, the kids visited the cemetery and sang a blazing "Happy Birthday"—obvious from the stubs of blue candles now littering the ground. I had noticed then how wax was encasing the porous granite. If the wax were left, Reed's artistic headstone would be permanently discolored.

What would Mother have done? Suddenly, I knew. I went home, boiled water, and returned, an hour later, to scrape wax from the headstone with a paring knife.

As I knelt to begin the restoration process, I was stunned by pain that gripped my left shoulder. I clamped it hard with my right hand, trying to alleviate the sharp stabs that drew air from my lungs like a syringe.

Suddenly I was sobbing. My body was gripped in a vise-like torture that came out of nowhere. The water spilled, the wax melted, and I bent over in shock. Where had this pain come from?

Fast-forward to my Rubenfeld Synergy training, the first week of November. We were working in pairs, and I partnered with Jane Whittaker, an insightful talk therapist from the East Coast. She sat to my left, facing my shoulder.

She cupped her hands gently on each side of my shoulder and softly inquired, "What are you noticing, Georgena?"

With that invitation to authentically listen to my body, the sharp, stabbing pain emerged like lava from an exploding volcano.

"Pain," I told her. "Pain as if a saber-toothed tiger is gripping my shoulder, ready to rip my arm off."

For a split second, I was embarrassed by my outburst. I returned my attention to the excruciating feelings in my left shoulder. Shock waves of agony were moving through the bone of my left scapula.

"Pain," Jane repeated. This repetition allowed me to hear my experience in my own words.

This technique increased my awareness as a trainee that the body tells the truth. It was up to me to listen. How often do we fail to hear the wisdom of our own words?

"Pain like a saber-toothed tiger," she continued.

Her hands began to move down my arm—and with them the pain.

My eyes flew open. "Jane. It's gone. The pain is gone." Jane's touch had released the pain and had begun to rewire my heart. Just like that, the pain had been released by this method of gentle Listening Touch.

I later learned from Noel Wight, of the Rubenfeld Training Institute, that it was my heart chakra that had exuded this grief.

The chakras are energy spots in the body. Each is described as a cone emerging from the body at specific points. The heart chakra extends from the top of the sternum to the bottom of the rib cage, and this was what encased my left scapula. The trauma of Reed's departure had not only been trapped in my diaphragm, but also in my heart.

I had just experienced the first principle of the Grief Relief workshop that I would develop a decade later: *Grief lives in one's body.*

This principle is obvious to health-care practitioners who care for grieving patients. Grief is revealed as a chronic cough. The lungs, in Chinese medicine, are considered to be the holding place for grief. Another indicator of stuck grief is a sinus blockage of the sixth chakra, the third eye, in the middle of the forehead.

As I began this training, I myself was stuck in Fragile Grief.

Truly, unprocessed grief is the hidden source of many of our bodies' issues. It can cause us to lose sleep, lack focus, get sick, age quickly, and lose motivation. Grief can keep on unwanted weight or diminish our health and vitality. It causes problems in our friendships, partnerships, and families. Yet people do not know that the root cause is unheard grief.

The second principle of the Grief Relief workshop naturally followed: *You've got to feel it to heal it.*

Scraping that candle wax from Reed's headstone was the first time I had felt my "embodied grief" in my left shoulder. I had felt the initial pain in my heart in those first ninety days after his death. But the excruciating stabbing in my shoulder was foreign until that day at the cemetery.

I finally began to listen to my body.

Throughout my adulthood, whenever I was stressed, my body would try to get my attention by growing polyps and fibroids. The first incident occurred when I was in college, attending Nebraska Wesleyan, a private liberal arts school where I was majoring in English. I faced a conflict when I chose a new major, speech-language pathology, which could not be awarded by my current school. I would have to transfer to our state university—and the thought frightened me. Nebraska Wesleyan was a safe, easy-to-navigate campus. The professors were brilliant, nurturing, and inspiring. I was in my comfort zone in a beautiful sorority house.

So, as I was taking up the practice of yoga overlooking the NWU campus each afternoon, a polyp was growing in the back of my nose. It was discovered when I fell asleep as a passenger and began snoring loudly on the way home for spring break. An exam by an astute ear, nose, and throat physician revealed a nearly four-inch growth that was blocking my airflow. The metaphor was clear. Not moving onto the next level of education was restricting the flow of my life. My fear was holding me back.

Even though I had fibroids removed in 1971 and another nasal polyp in 1975, I still did not learn to listen to my body.

As a teenager, I had put on weight perfecting my baking skills as a 4-H member. My angel food and sponge cakes earned purple ribbons at the Nebraska State Fair. My dad and brothers began to call me "Nebraska Fats" as my thighs and butt ballooned. Even though this was typical shape-changing for a girl entering puberty, my mother did not educate them.

We were a family of less-than-kind nicknames. Mark was Stinky Jones, sung to the tune of driving a locomotive around the bend. Alan, when he began to stutter in ninth grade, earned the name Shoshone. I had no idea how these words of ridicule were creating trauma in my body.

There was no invasive surgery, sexual assault, or violent car wreck. And yet the trauma was just as real. Name-calling was an under-the-radar assault on my self-worth, and I wasn't even aware of it. It was bullying.

The body that had housed my dancing spirit as a three-year-old and then as a gracious adult pleaser became my enemy as I grew older. I hated the way I looked. I began using self-talk to blame myself for not doing enough and to shame myself because I was not enough. I was fat.

I began a diet roller coaster that continued into my late twenties. I was not kind to myself; I did not drink when I was thirsty, sleep when I was tired, or eat when I needed energy.

And then I received a gift. Dad had a quadruple heart bypass in 1978, which helped him, and all of us in the family, shift to mindful eating.

Out with the Jell-O and whipped toppings. In with broccoli and salads. I began to take supplements and read about alternative treatments. Yet I still had much to learn when it came to listening to the body.

When Reed was born, he had colic. At six months, he developed ear infections. Although I nursed him and loved holding him, I was sleep-deprived. Even though tubes were put in his ears at nine months, I still felt out of control. That spring, a lump was discovered in my breast, but thankfully, it was just a plugged milk gland. Even so, my stress mounted. I simply did not get things done. I could not even make the bed each day.

The stress of what was *not* happening nagged at me.

And then, in the fall of that year, a lump was discovered in my thyroid. The deep truth was that I had lost my ability to speak up—but this was not a truth I understood at the time. I did not even tell my parents about my surgery. I simply scheduled it and told no one except Edward and the babysitter. I was in and out of the hospital and back to work as a speech pathologist in a few days. My voice was hoarse. I wore a scarf around my neck. I pushed through the fatigue of anesthesia lingering in my body.

Even though the lump was gone, my inability to speak up remained. No wonder a thick rope-like scar formed. Something had to remind me of the danger of my Type A behavior as this driven thirty-something.

Now I believe that, even in the womb, Reed's sensitive soul absorbed our family trait of shame. Further, all my doubts and pressures that year passed through my milk into Reed. I continued to drive myself, oblivious, not at all attuned to the body-mind connection.

It was the *aha* of Synergy training that allowed me to look back at my medical history and begin to understand what had been happening. My body had tried to defend itself from my numbing pace by developing sacs filled with toxins.

Discovering my connection to my mind-body wisdom I begin to ask:

Is there a place in my body that consistently calls for attention: an ache, a pain?

I rub my hands together and bring them apart until I can't feel the heat or energy between them. It feels like I am pulling taffy. I bring them back together and rub them again until the heat/energy returns.

Now I float one or more hands onto that place or those places in my body that are calling for attention. My left shoulder is usually aching because this is where grief lives.

I simply notice what is happening beneath my hands.

I am present to myself. There is no right or wrong answer. I suspend self-judgment, one of the benefits of this gentle, miraculous process of Listening Touch.

Discovering the Gift of the Rubenfeld Synergy Method®

NOVEMBER 1998–JUNE 2002

Life was not turning out the way I had envisioned. The harder I worked to do and be good, the worse things seemed to get. I was still loving others, but not myself.

My son was dead.

In my Fragile Grief, I blamed myself.

I'd lived my life brimming with judgment and self-criticism.

There were tears just under the surface of everything.

I was stuck in my Fragile Grief and had no way out. My morning spiritual ritual was my lifeline.

Life was better; I was only crying for minutes, now. Still, I did not feel alive. I felt lonely, frustrated, and sad most of the time.

I began the Rubenfeld Synergy Method® training November 1, 1998. I arrived in Orillia, Canada, tightly wound. I felt compelled to learn this healing process.

I was barely holding myself together. To the untrained eye, I looked fine. My hair and clothes were perfect for every activity. I had tights and yoga tops for lying on the floor during our body-mind exercises. I had scarves and dangly earrings for Saturday Night Live skits. I pulled my hair back, revealing my inner state. Tight.

Fragile Grief is like this. I could appear put-together outwardly, which was a relief to family and friends. They could assume I was "healing." And yet, with just a thought, I could be pulled into the vortex of deep, dark grief. My feelings of sadness seemed eternal. I wanted people to say

Reed's name, yet it often released my tears. I felt afraid that this Fragile Grief would never end. It now felt like a dragon, draggin' me around.

It was my mother's birthday. Mother had told my cousin Peggy, "Don't tell Georgena anything more about this Therapeutic Touch. She will want to stop being a speech pathologist and do it, too." She knew this work would hold a magnetic attraction for me. As a Certified Rubenfeld Synergist, I would be communicating with people at not only the level of words, tone, and body language, but with body wisdom, energy, and the soul self. She saw this as a "woo-woo" modality then. If only she had known that research in the twenty-first century would validate the power of touch to heal trauma and rewire the mind-heart-gut-brain.

Now we each stood before the community to introduce ourselves. Ours was the largest training class ever, with fifty-four students and fourteen faculty. I knew only one other person, my friend Diane Marie Blinn, who had "accidentally" signed up and taken Ilana's workshop a year earlier. It was Diane who had sat beside me on our couch when she got home, sharing her joy over the experience.

"I have found my teacher," she said. "Ilana Rubenfeld will teach me to listen with my hands and to support people to tell their story while the emotions are released from their body. I experienced more shifts in a week than in years of talk therapy! It may very well be the training for you to become a better listener in a completely new way."

Diane's visit was just weeks before Reed's death.

Now, this first Sunday of the training, I wore a long black sweater with the outline of an eagle in brown suede. It had been purchased in Vail, Colorado, on our last family skiing trip. There, Reed had rounded a corner too fast and plowed into a ski school of snow bunnies. The ski instructor had angrily warned him that his recklessness would not be tolerated. If there was another incident, his lift ticket would be removed.

"Slow down," I kept telling Reed, when he was a grade-schooler. He'd race across a wet floor, fall, and hit his head. I feared that one day he'd come away with a head injury. During my work at Shock Trauma, I'd seen serious consequences result from even a mild bump on the head.

One woman had slipped on the ice, hit the back of her head, and arrived to the Shock Trauma Center on a Sunday evening. I had given her our diagnostic protocol Monday morning and not detected any deficits in her responses. She returned a week later reporting that she was having excruciating headaches, screaming at her children, and needing to stay in a darkened room. Life could change so quickly, I had learned while working there.

When Reed became a teenager with raging hormones, I did not repeat the lesson to "slow down." I myself had never modeled what it was to slow down and live in a healthy way, and I was not going down the road of "do as I say and not as I do."

Speed was destroying us. Indeed, less than ninety minutes had elapsed between the ringing phone call from the school and the single shot ringing out.

Slowing down and listening was simply not the way I lived. I would quickly discover this was my "growing edge' to learn gentle Listening Touch. Over and over during the four-year training, I would hear this invitation from my beloved supervisors to a new pattern of being. "Slow down" they would whisper as they stood behind me as mentors. "Listen and trust your inner wisdom."

And yet it was something I, myself, had cried out for. There had been one morning, meeting with a group of dynamic women in Norfolk, when I suddenly said out loud, "I wonder what it would be like to be a better listener?" The words came rushing through me like a Nebraska twister. "I have never had a class in listening in all my training as a speech-language pathologist," I added.

And now, beginning the training, I could feel the giddy residual of those words.

It was Diane who helped me navigate international travel from Norfolk to Toronto. It was Diane who was my roommate during those first three modules. She sat with me as witness as I processed my guilt. It was Diane who knew of my loss, which I would reveal to only a handful of my fellow trainees. It was Diane who had written and, in a heartfelt way, delivered Reed's eulogy.

Making eye contact first with Diane, I stood up to introduce myself, feeling so at ease in this room of strangers. I had the odd sensation we had all met before.

"I want to thank my husband, Edward," I began, "and my son, Vincent, for their support of my decision to begin this training. I feel as though I am standing on the edge a cliff, ready to step off and be fully supported to fly."

Reed had gone through his "eagle" phase, drawing the majestic bird perched as a wise watcher, soaring above detailed landscapes. How surprising that I was dressed in this costume tonight, speaking of flying.

The next morning, I showed up to hear Ilana outline the process of our training in her pioneer Rubenfeld Synergy Method (RSM®):

1. Begin with beginner's mind—a sense of discovery and curiosity.
2. Set your intention for the client and for yourself using gentle Listening Touch.
3. Be present, and never ever leave your client, mentally, physically, emotionally or energetically.

Thinking back, I realize how much was left unsaid. This method was a body-mind therapy, an educational paradigm to empower people to heal themselves by connecting with their bodies through gentle Listening Touch. They would learn to listen to and trust their bodies. Confidence would fill the core of their being. This method allows for the release of their traumatic emotions as the 'story' of their life is told.

Now that I am a Synergist, I understand it also as a truly spiritual process where I hold the highest and best for my clients. I am not there to fix them, because there is nothing to fix. I see their perfection. It is their Soul Selves, their inner Golden Buddhas that will be revealed beneath their limiting beliefs, habitual behavior patterns, attitudes, and values.

As Synergist, it is my responsibility to be as clear as possible about my habitual, unconscious patterns. Awareness is curative. It is essential that I do my work to claim my worth.

As the four-year training began, my fellow trainees and I began removing our clay prisons with myriad personal synergy sessions.

The first time I heard the story of the Golden Buddha was from Eve Hogan, a gifted teacher on the island of Maui. In 1957, a group of Tibetan monks were informed that a highway was being built through their shrine. The huge clay Buddha in the shrine would have to be moved.

Arrangements were made, and the day of moving the Buddha arrived. As the crane began lifting the clay Buddha off of its block, its resting place, it began to crack. It was far heavier than all the engineers had estimated. The monk supervising the movement of the Buddha frantically called to the crane operator to tell him to set the Buddha down. Quickly, the alert crane operator carefully lowered the Buddha onto the ground.

As the monks and engineers examined the Buddha, they found several large cracks. A larger crane would be needed, but one could not be brought until the next day. The Buddha would have to spend the night in its current unprotected location. To make matters worse, a storm was coming.

The monks covered the Buddha with waterproof tarps on poles to keep it dry overnight. All seemed to be well. During the night, the head monk, awakened by the sound of the rain, arose to check on the Buddha. With a flashlight, the monk carefully checked the statue's condition. As he walked around the huge clay figure, shining his light on the cracks, something caught his eye. He looked closely, peering into the crack. What he saw he did not understand. He needed to see more. He went back to his quarters, found a chisel and a hammer and returned to the Buddha. He began carefully chipping at the clay around the crack. As the crack widened, he could not believe his eyes. He ran to wake the other monks and instructed each to bring hammer and chisel. By lantern light, the monks carefully chipped all the clay from the Buddha.

After hours of chiseling, the monks stepped back and stared in awe at the sight before them. There, in front of the monks, stood a solid gold Buddha.

When the moving crew arrived later that morning to complete the job of moving the Buddha to its new location, there was much confusion and excitement. Where had the clay Buddha gone? From where had the Golden Buddha come? Historians were consulted as the monks began to investigate the origin of the Golden Buddha.

It was discovered that the Golden Buddha was the cherished responsibility of a group of monks several centuries earlier. These monks received word that the Burmese army was headed their way. Concerned that the invading army would loot the shrine for its Golden Buddha, the monks covered their Buddha with eight to twelve inches of clay. When they were finished, the Golden Buddha appeared to be a Buddha of clay. The invading army would surely have no interest.

The monks were right. The invading army had no reason to take this Buddha as loot. They did, however, kill all the monks before they moved on. So the truth lay dormant for centuries until the Buddha cracked during this final move, and gold shone through the cracks.

Each of us is like a Golden Buddha with an energy system of meridians that runs like deep, wide rivers through the body. Many sensitive individuals, like Reed, enter our world with ease. And yet they can experience energy blocks immediately, from the trauma of the bright light of the delivery room, the fear of the people around them, or the lack of nourishment. Reed's colic was a symptom of such a blockage.

Many ancient modalities, such as acupuncture and yoga, support the dislodging of these blocks so the body can return to its natural state of flow. The body knows how to heal itself, returning to healthy balance. During a Synergy session, our energy will begin to flow freely once we feel safe and trust the Synergist. We can tell our story, a result of the direct or indirect trauma we have experienced.

A Synergist offers support with gentle Listening Touch to release the emotions of that story held in the body. When our Golden Buddha selves are revealed through self-care, acceptance, self-love, and reconnection with the body's wisdom, the clay of false beliefs, outdated values, and toxic attitudes will crumble. As the client, I will replace them with my own new, empowering beliefs embedded at the cellular level with the support of my Synergist. As Synergist to my clients, I will hold that sacred space as they discover what they want to have happen in their lives. I will repeat their verbal affirmations and guide them to integrate new ways of being. It is a transformational process for those with trauma and grief stuck in their bodies.

But in the beginning of my training, I knew none of this.

Inwardly, I said *yes* to the beginner's mind, not knowing "how to do it." I was unaware that I was a Golden Buddha myself and would support others in that self-discovery.

I felt excitement for the adventure before me. Yet I still needed to learn how to move beyond my grief.

I had begun my grief journey in the darkness, returning home from the hospital that January morning facing the greatest loss of my life. I had yet to grasp these truths:

1. Loss is a part of life. It is going to happen to everyone.
2. Everything living moves into another form. Even our children depart.
3. There is a part of us that never dies. That Essence will live on in another dimension.
4. Grief is transformative when we allow it to be. It does not have to be a dragon draggin' us around for years. We can transcend it.

Presence as a Gift in Grief

NOVEMBER 4, 1998

I was midway through week one of a twelve-week training. I had seen some heart-wrenching community sessions in the past few days. One woman released a flood of emotions at Ilana's touch. These emotions had been frozen in her body at age seven as she cared for her mother, who was bedridden with multiple sclerosis. She was ensnared by the poverty the disease had created.

A second woman asserted her preference for romance with other women—coming out of the closet to experience the safe container of our community. A third woman took on the grace of a beautiful swan, transformed as she accessed her creative self-longing to emerge. Each session overflowed with tears of sadness, fear, and joy. As witness, I was stunned.

One evening, Ilana gave instructions for the next day. Volunteers should dress in color for the camera, she told us. Everything would be videotaped.

In the morning, I felt drawn to a striking forest-green top and leggings. *Huh!* I thought. *I wonder why I'm choosing this.* Going by intuition was not my usual mode. I acted on impulse without forethought or consideration of the consequences. That day, I felt calm, with a knowing beyond the five senses. My Fragile Grief was not draggin' me around in that moment. I noticed and was so grateful.

I had bought all new, comfortable clothes for the trip, suitable for hours on chairs or in back-jacks or lying on padded tables. Yet this was the outfit that spoke to me. My Synergy session in front of the entire community had already begun, only I did not know it.

A faint smile flitted across my lips like a sunrise cloud as I dressed at that early hour of the day.

"It is essential that you never ever leave your client, physically, mentally, or emotionally," Ilana charged us as we gathered in the whale-sized room. Windows framed the southern forest beyond, flooding this sacred space with sunlight. "Always stay present," she added.

And then Ilana said, "Today I want two volunteers. One to be Synergist, and one to be client. I will supervise the session."

My hand shot up when I heard the word "client." Intention or impulsivity? My rational brain had not registered the "why" of this choice. Perhaps that is what Reed experienced that night. I may never know.

Approaching the table with "beginner's mind," I sat on the edge with my hands folded in the perfect "S" curve I'd learned in finishing school. It was my protection to look put-together. I felt scared. I was being seen by the entire community. *What had I gotten myself into?*

"Lie down," began the symphony conductor. *How many sessions has she begun with these two simple words? I wonder.*

"Camilla," she directed the volunteer. "Place your hands on Georgena's head for First Touch." Camilla's fingers gently contacted the base of my skull. She carefully cupped her palms around the bony helmet protecting my brain. I felt the loving touch of a mother supporting her infant.

"What are you noticing, Georgena?" Camilla asked, her voice soothing.

"I am relaxed," I replied, sinking into the support of the table, with Camilla's hands on the back of my head holding me.

How often in life had I longed to be held in this safe, gentle way?

Camilla moved to my feet, placed her palms on the outside edge of each foot, and asked "What are you noticing?"

Once again, her touch conveyed safety. Camilla was merely hearing with gentle Listening Touch what was going on in my body. Two simple hand placements, on my head and feet, had put my busy, ever-vigilant brain at ease. The mind chatter ceased. The emotional part of my brain, the limbic system, could now be accessed. I sank deeper into the support of the table.

After this simple session, I would be able to re-create this feeling of safety and security any time I chose. Instead of being coiled like a Slinky, ready to spew energy into the places and spaces of others, I could melt like butter, releasing my usual pattern of tension.

This educational paradigm had quick results, I noted. I felt it in my body, grateful. I took a breath, still not full because of the block in my diaphragm, but with less effort.

I answered Camilla, "My right foot is pointed at a forty-five-degree angle, while my left foot is straight, pointing up."

"Open your eyes, put your hands behind your head, and look at your feet," Ilana instructed. I did so, discovering that my description was correct. This was educating me, the client, to know that I was connected to my body.

I had disassociated from my body more than thirty years ago when I was labeled "Nebraska Fats." Now I was empowered. We were less than fifteen minutes into the session.

"Georgena is a keen observer," Ilana reported to Camilla.

After all those years of observing my clients, I was slowing down and observing myself. The safety of the session deepened. I felt both protected by Ilana and Camilla and connected to the love expanding my heart.

"Now, Camilla," Ilana directed, "place your hands there in the knee cradle." Ilana's tone softened as she stood by Camilla's right shoulder. With my eyes closed, I brought my attention to my right knee. I felt a slight pressure and warmth. Camilla's hand on my knee felt cool. An image flashed before me.

"What are you noticing in your knee, Georgena?" Camilla queried.

"Dark clouds," I responded as an image of dense, charcoal-gray clouds appeared in my mind's eye.

Camilla jerked back her hands.

"What happened, Camilla?" Ilana's inquiry was gentle.

"I was scared, so I pulled my hands away."

Ilana smiled. "That is an example of why you will be trained to never, ever leave your clients, no matter what comes up," she said. "Where they go, you will go. Thank you, Camilla," she added, without any note of judgment. "You were the perfect Synergist."

Ilana started clapping and the class joined in. I opened my eyes, smiled, and winked at Ilana, knowing that even though these clouds were dark, they were only clouds and would float away like emotions. They were nothing compared with what I had seen in my mind's eye during the past ten months.

Ilana said, "Close your eyes, Georgena," and placed her hands around that right knee once again. "What are you noticing now?"

"The clouds are less dark," I answered. "They are starting to move." Ilana repeated my observations word for word. This technique of reflection deepened the experience of what I was seeing.

"The peak of a mountain is breaking through," I continued. "It's covered with snow." Ilana verbally reflected.

"The sun is starting to appear in the upper-right-hand corner of this scene," I went on.

"Tell me more about the mountain, Georgena."

"It is very tall, snowcapped, amethyst-purple, with a granite base."

After precisely reflecting, Ilana asked, "And if that mountain had a voice, what would it say?"

"It is beautiful. It is wise."

"Can you change that, Georgena, to 'I am beautiful?'" the master conductor asked.

"I am beautiful," I said. "Now the sun is starting to melt the snow, and water is streaming down the mountain." I could feel warmth flowing from the top of my head, through my body, and out my feet. That powerful, Peaceful Presence had returned.

"*I am beautiful.* This session could be entitled 'Knee to Life,'" she offered.

In closing, Ilana invited me to open my eyes, sit, and repeat the affirmation: "I am beautiful." Every cell of my body said, "*Yes!*" I would begin to see beauty everywhere in my outer world as my sense of my inner beauty grew over time. Beauty was to be one of the healing tools of my grief journey. It was a gift from the wisdom of my body.

She gestured for me to step down onto the earth. So much had happened with just three simple, powerful moves. I felt a deep connection with the floor as I returned to my place in the circle. No wonder I had been drawn to the forest-green outfit, as pines forested the base of my mountain. The image of the mountain resonated with many. Joyce offered to draw the mountain on my square canvas tote bag. Others came up to share their experiences.

They, too, felt the power of this mountain arise and could sense themselves anchored safely in the moment. What the one in the center of the community experiences ripples out to many. I would experience this phenomenon over the next four years.

A class of new trainees joined us in March 1999. They had watched the videos of the November training. Several of them, meeting me for the first time, said, "We thought you were faking your session. It was not a loud, explosive emotional release as with the others." I smiled and thanked them for sharing.

Little did they know that this mountain image, so sacred in many native cultures, was my grounding force. The tsunami of grief would dash me to the depths of despair whenever I allowed myself to return to the thought of how I had not taken Reed's hand. It was this image and the embodied sense of that mountain within my knee that would save me from guilt and shame. I would repeat "I am beautiful" and begin to feel it emerging as a tiny seed in my heart.

I would see, feel, and breathe in its power within me. The excruciating pain of Fragile Grief would dissipate in an instant whenever I shifted my thought from the night of that perfect storm night to the gift of this majestic mountain, feeling it in my knee.

The purpose of that session was to demonstrate staying present to our clients. How perfect that it was that the grounded image of a mountain, floating from behind dark clouds, had appeared not only for me, but for everyone in the community in that moment.

What is more present than a mountain?

I was living in Nebraska at the time. My fellow trainees would ask, "Have you found your mountain yet?" They could feel that indeed this mountain existed somewhere on the planet. A move to Fort Collins in

2000 and a trip to the Grand Tetons in 2001 did not reveal the actual amethyst peak.

Not until the spring of 2003, after living in Portland, Oregon for seven months, did I gaze at Mount Hood shimmering in the morning light. Suddenly I realized, *this is the mountain in my knee!* I had been looking at her beauty for months, and I had not recognized my anchor, my beautiful sacred mountain.

How often was the right answer towering ahead of me, but I simply did not recognize it? What if I greeted grief with curiosity and discovery instead of sadness and fear?

Indeed, my grief journey would be eased when I shifted my thoughts to this mountain and felt its presence throughout my body. I had a magnificent resource to move beyond my grief.

Discovering the Gift of Beauty with Grounding and Gratitude

NOVEMBER–DECEMBER 1998

I returned to Nebraska with a sense of beauty within myself, the healing reconnection from that sacred table with Ilana.

Of course it did not last forever, but I could return to the peaceful, powerful Presence immediately by imagining the mountain image and sensations. I could feel the ripples moving through me. My body, the sacred temple of God within, was now becoming more alive. How often it is that we find God in the moment, if we only return.

I was an unusual griever, for I never got angry with God or Reed. I had sensed that Reed's death was bigger than both of us. I knew that God would always be with me, even as I turned away from God and then returned, again and again.

Somehow I knew that I would move through this Fragile Grief, inspiring others with the tools I was discovering as a pioneer of self-care, object permanence, curiosity, and Listening Touch.

Now that I had completed this first module of Synergy training, I could finally focus on myself. Before the training, it had been a long, long time since I had been able to feel anything but exhaustion and sadness or feeling overwhelmed. I had been walking in dense fog on an iceberg that was breaking apart beneath my feet; such was the vast ocean of my sorrow. I could not see my way.

Now, during my sunrise walks among the trees on the golf course, things were very different. The holidays were nearly upon me, and winter was fast approaching in Nebraska, yet I felt safe. I was home within my body. I could tap into the eternal spirit, my essence.

Throughout the previous spring and summer, Reed had sent us miraculous gifts of monarch and swallowtail butterflies. It was as if he was assuring us: life *is* good and beautiful.

It started with Edward's grief odyssey, on a day he took an early spring morning run. He never ran the same course two days in a row because he craved variety. One warm spring morning, running beside a row of pines on the north edges of the Norfolk Country Club, he slowed to rest. Looking up, he saw a swallowtail butterfly gliding through the branches. It immediately reminded him of the butterfly card Reed had created for that elementary fundraiser that now seemed so long ago.

Edward froze, deepened his breathing, and carefully stretched his arm in front of him. With open palm inviting connection, he waited. The butterfly hovered at eye-level, then came to rest in his hand. For a long instant, it was as if Reed had returned to say "Hi, Dad." Then the butterfly resumed its journey, no longer visible to his eye, but forever uplifting his heart.

The butterfly begins life as a fuzzy fat caterpillar that eats and eats and eats its way into oblivion. Then it spins a dark, hard cocoon, its chrysalis, around itself. Within this protection, transformation occurs.

But first, within the chrysalis, the caterpillar must turn to soup. All sense of its former self is lost. In this dark place, there floats up and out and into this soup imaginal cells. They portend what is to come. At first, they are just glimmers from which the butterfly will form and emerge.

So it was that I connected with the earth on those November days while still in the soup of Fragile Grief. The person I had been was decimated. I was encased in darkness in the hard cocoon. Yet I could glimpse who I might become. I could feel myself one day emerging from this grief and stepping into full aliveness. Oh yes, I would be internally beautiful, for this truth now lived in my bones. "I am beautiful" was the affirmation I repeated often, lifting myself out of grief's despair.

Once again, I would be strong enough to migrate thousands of miles, so fragile that a slight tear of my wings could ground me from ever soaring again. This awareness filled me with compassion for each and every soul walking the planet. We are all created to be courageous, focused potential. We have irrepressible spirits, even when terrible things happen.

We are wounded, and sometimes, we never fly again.

I was now ten months into my grief odyssey. The first Easter, Mother's Day, and Reed's birthday had passed. How did I want to honor Reed on Thanksgiving and Christmas? The choice was mine to create new rituals with Edward and Vincent.

We all sat down to begin creating our "new now" holiday traditions. I convened the family meeting by saying, "The holidays are coming. We cannot escape them. What are they going to look like this year?"

We had very little energy. Vincent was just completing his first semester at Hastings College. Edward and I had returned to the business of running a rehab agency serving twenty nursing homes and four rural hospitals. We were all fatigued to the max. Yet we all needed to show up for the rest of the Kuzma clan. Even though the holidays would bring back memories of good times, it was clear that things would never be the same.

We talked about Thanksgiving, Mother's favorite holiday. She would gather her entire family around a table graced by a gorgeous centerpiece she'd created of flowers, fruit, and nuts.

"We feel like nuts right now," I said, and Edward and Vincent both laughed.

Soon after that, my brother, Alan, volunteered to host the clan for Thanksgiving in Lincoln.

What a blessing it was. Everyone could drive to his centrally located home, always a welcoming place. We would each bring our favorite food, and he would cook the turkey, mash ten pounds of potatoes, and enlist Vincent to make gourmet gravy. We invited Aunt Dell, who had just celebrated her ninetieth birthday. She was the sage and keeper of Edward's family history.

So it was on a beautiful, sunny, sixty-degree day, we gathered to celebrate the blessing of family for the first time without Dad and Reed. It would be the one and only time that Alan would ever have all of us for Thanksgiving, together with Reed's cousins, aunts, uncles, father, brother, and mother. We gave thanks for health, each other, and the energy to keep putting one foot in front of the other.

It was my responsibility to make the dressing and the centerpiece. Each were hallmarks of Mother's creativity. Instead of Mother's fruits, nuts, and mums, I brought in pheasant feathers for each family member we had lost, from Mark, to Mother, to Reed. A new tradition had begun. With sadness and gratitude, we encircled the table, each in turn sharing who they were missing and what gift that person had given.

Of course, everyone missed Grandma Betty's homemade rolls, even though Alan had gotten up at the crack of dawn to make nearly identical ones.

I was glad that we had planned ahead for the challenges. The changes we made allowed for the semblance of past Thanksgiving traditions. It did not feel as if we were celebrating a foreign tradition. Yet we did not try to do it all.

Later in the afternoon, Aunt Della fell asleep in the sun in one of Alan's wing-backed chairs. Cousins Daniel, Michael, and Vincent, pranksters that they were, wanted to verify that her motionless self had not departed. Putting a mirror beneath her nose, they could barely contain their laughter as her exhalations fogged the surface.

We would confess to her as tears flowed down our faces, this time in happiness, not sorrow.

I would later learn in my training that laughter can lighten and enlighten during a Synergy session. It can dissolve fear, free tight holding patterns in the body, and create pathways to creativity, insight, and healing. As a Synergist, I know that humor and the resulting laughter can provide the psychological oxygen we require, just as a dolphin takes a deep gulp of air before it dives deeper.

This holiday was one of peaceful mourning. The sadness that pervaded my bones was palpable. Yet knowing and honoring that, we could establish the ability to have a joyous Thanksgiving in the years to come. This truth kept me going.

I had a choice. I could continue to dwell on the thoughts: Reed is gone; this is not the way life is supposed to be; was this really his time to go; why didn't I take his hand? Or I could embrace the possibility that indeed Reed's departure was the radical shift that I had needed, the shift that would transform me from my cocoon of grief, beyond my imagination.

I began to see beauty everywhere. Although I had always loved flowers, trees, and children, I had never realized the power of beauty. Even the interplay of light and shadows on the grass in the morning became a thing of beauty for me.

I began to look in the mirror and see myself differently. "I am beautiful," I could whisper. Like most women, I was unable to say the words aloud, yet every day my voice grew stronger. What I knew to be true and good was that God would see me through. As I was seeking beauty, it would be everywhere within my sight.

Edward, Vincent, and I sat down after Thanksgiving, keeping in mind our family motto: "Every problem has a manageable solution." Our next challenge was Christmas.

Vincent blurted, "Let's get out of town to someplace warm."

We knew that traveling would help us cope with our recent loss.

We sat and each thought about where people were that we loved. "What about our friends the Smiths in Arizona?" Vincent offered.

As it turned out, this family graciously, courageously opened their home and welcomed us for Christmas. Since Vincent had grown up with the Smith boys, we rightly discerned that this would be active and exciting, yet not overwhelming.

We were aware. We could not escape the holidays, but with God, all things were possible. We would mourn intentionally, planning where we would be and with whom, allowing whatever feelings emerged to be felt. Crying openly and laughing heartily at a funny memory.

Our "new now" then, this first Christmas without Reed's earthly presence, was all about supportive friendships.

Our thoughtful family discussion helped us to decide:

- What did we want to feel and experience?
- What traditions would we keep?
- What traditions would be placed on hold this year?
- What new traditions that would evoke fun and laughter would evolve?
- Where would we celebrate?
- All of these things would be our choice.

The First Anniversary

꼭◎ ◎ꙮ

T he date was fast approaching on the calendar. It could not be denied, hidden, or skipped. I had made it through all the other "firsts," and there were surprises and gifts in each.

On February 9, 1998, my forth-eighth birthday, I survived, thanks to the love of family and friends who sent a plethora of cards and flowers. At the heart of each greeting was an "I love you." That was truly what this grief saga was all about. I was learning to love myself in spite of my failure to take Reed's hand. I would soon learn that listening to my body and responding with self-care was the first of my three steps to self-love.

Palm Sunday had brought the palpable presence of Reed and Mother in the dream and then with the two orbs of light. It was as if these were two candles whose flames began to dissipate grief's darkness. For me, my despair lightened with these two lights. A sliver of hope returned.

Mother's Day had been remarkably calm. I was working on the completion of Vincent's T-shirt quilt. There were thirty squares, including one with the Dukes of Hazard T-shirt Vincent had worn as a six-year-old. The lower left row of the quilt held the Batman shirt that Reed had created with puff paint for Vincent's ninth birthday, when we lived in Baltimore. The finishing touch was Vincent's number forty senior football jersey. It was a montage of his life.

Sitting in the quiet of the living room, I whip-stitched the border. At the same moment, I did not understand how I had been whipping myself with guilt for nearly four months.

Moving to the golf course side of the room, I could not believe my eyes. There, out in the garden, among the brilliant pink, red, and orange tulips I had planted in the fall, was a white one, taller than the rest. Of course, the practical among my friends just rolled their eyes upon hearing the story. "There she goes again, interpreting the everyday as a sign from Reed." For me, this tulip dispelled more despair.

On July 27, 1998, Reed's sixteenth birthday, our celebration had revealed grief gripping my left shoulder like a saber-toothed tiger as I cleaned his headstone. This experience would be the headstone of my belief, teaching me that we *can* move through grief.

The truth is that we don't want to acknowledge grief, let alone provide the time, compassion, or support to explore how it lives in the body. As a culture, we don't discuss moving through it. We just want to get it over with as quickly as possible. When the grief goes on "too long," people become uncomfortable. The griever is given medication "so all those feelings won't be a problem." The grief talk, about us as a country avoiding this inevitable process, is long overdue.

Thanksgiving 1998 brought the gifts of gathering at Alan's, the new and improved centerpiece, and the Aunt Della prank, which gave us stories to recount annually with laughter.

Now we faced a choice. January 23 was approaching. Thankfully, it would not be a Friday night, for Friday nights had taken on a deep sadness for us. Diane Blinn had invited us over to be with her and her husband, Gary on January 30, that very first Friday night. She'd had the insight to know being out of the house until after 10 p.m. would support our healing.

Now the upcoming Reed's Day, as I had named it, could not be ignored. Reed's friends had already begun asking what we were going to do.

I called the school officials with a proposal. We would bring the talented Pippa White, an actress from Lincoln, to educate students about the settlement of the prairie. Her one-woman show, *The Orphan Train,* would be performed at the Norfolk Senior High for Reed's sophomore class and the fifth and sixth graders of Northern Hills Elementary, where he had thrived.

I dutifully submitted my idea to the director of student services. Everyone knew that this assembly would be financed with Reed's memorial funds. Those monies had poured from the hearts of people all over the state and had already financed a garden on the cross country track at Sky View Lake. Yet the school administrators kept up a fearful undercurrent. Too much attention on Reed might result in another death. My words had to be approved, words meant to acknowledge the purpose of the gathering and to celebrate each of the students for their courage and resilience the past year in moving through their grief.

The school officials didn't know about the letters I'd answered, reaching out to students who said Reed had saved their lives.

The students leaned forward in their seats as their gaze followed Pippa from train station to corn field to the farmhouse for orphans who came to prairie homes. The questions that followed buoyed my heart as students wanted to know more about this part of their Midwest history.

On Friday night, we had dozens of teens for a lasagna dinner and birthday cake. The previous year, Reed's death on January 24, was one of sadness. Now that day had become Reed's Day. Tonight we celebrated Reed and also honored the sixteenth birthdays of his friends with *joy*.

Now I could look back. The year of "firsts" was complete. I had been present to each experience, discovering the gift. It had not been easy to face my fear that Reed would be forgotten. I struggled to remember that I was not alone as a grieving parent. Others had walked this path before me, and thousands would follow. I was grateful to be moving through the year.

Looking back on the year, I realized that Raw Grief had lasted nearly ninety days. Edward and I had made the choice to stop crying for days in late March. My hope returned with the dream and the orbs of light on Palm Sunday.

I would remain in Fragile Grief for years, though, because of my guilty thoughts. Where was the Grief Guide to remind me that each time I chose guilt, I was choosing self-loathing?

PART III

A New Mourning: Consciously Living the Gifts

A New Mourning: Why? How? What?

JANUARY 1999

S o here I was, a year after Reed's sudden, violent departure, still overwhelmed at what had happened. Vincent said to me, "A perceived step backward is simply preparation for a huge leap forward." I stepped back, looking to see where I stood now.

I had been looking within and without for answers. Believing that we are all interconnected, I saw my part in Reed's shame. It was time to forgive myself for not knowing his life plan. In my Fragile Grief, I was stuck in the repetitive cycle of belief that Reed should not have passed.

Wasn't it I who had said the night before in a meeting, "We never know …"? My soul knew the future on some level; the rest of me had been unwilling or unable to know. What if my son was one of those who came with the plan to stay for only a little while? Could I accept this truth?

The fact was, I was not consulted in the bigger picture. My sadness continued. I felt tormented by its constant presence. I wanted it to go away. My mind would then begin to spin like a top until I remembered that I had a choice. I could stay in the vortex of depressing grief or choose a new direction, a brave new mourning. In the traditional sense, mourning is an outward, cultural expression of grief. Wearing black for a specified number of days is the most common observance. Yet grief, bereavement, grieving, weeping, lamentation all come up when Googling mourning.

America: the land of the free and home of the brave. But are we really free when grief is lurking in our shadows as individuals and as a society? Are we really free when we are terrified to recognize where grief lives in our individual traumatized bodies? Are we brave enough as a culture to finally bring grief to the table for a thoughtful conversation? It is neither healthy nor efficient to stay on the accepted path of the rugged individualist who grieves alone.

Each of us experiences grief in our own way and on our own timeline. Grief is individual to every person. Many who have grieved deeply may choose to return to life with a new purpose and direction because of their loss. Time and again, in our community of Norfolk, parents of the same "grieving club" have created educational programs, memorials, and new careers after the sudden suicidal departure of their child.

Yet, in a sense, we have all been doing grief the old-fashioned way. The way of these old beliefs which are actually harmful myths:

1. *My heart will always have this wound. I will never be happy again.* (Most often the mantra of those in Fragile Grief)
2. *My grief and mourning should be focused on my departed. Self-care is selfish.* My clients appear with illness because they are neglecting themselves.
3. *I must do grief alone. No one can possibly understand the pain I am going through. No good can come from grief and loss.* (And: "*I would never see a Grief Guide. It would do no good.*") These are the comments I receive from concerned family members who see their loved ones becoming negative and withdrawn.
4. *My departed is gone. If I stop longing for my departed, I may forget or dishonor him or her.*

A more relevant model of grief would acknowledge:

- The body is an instrument that moves us confidently through grief when we learn to listen to its messages and welcome our feelings.
- Self-care is the foundation of moving through grief.

- Despair can move to curiosity with an intentional shift. Grief can be transformative. We can reinvent ourselves as a result of this grief.
- Object permanence is a sound principle to shift the longing of the griever to the confidence that the beloved continues to live on and communicate from the other side. We are really all One.

These truths have been left out the discussion, particularly the need for self-care. The griever must be given permission by family, friends, and place of business to shift healthful attention to self instead of the departed. This permission should extend for the entire first year.

My experience of my own grief is grueling when I:

- Do not care for myself and only care for others; disregarding Divine guidance, I force myself to keep doing for others at work and at home
- Fearfully resist my feelings, whether a morning cloud of sadness or grief triggered by guilty, angry, you-name-it thoughts
- Do not recognize the trauma and grief in my body, pushing it away without awareness
- Long for Reed

I want to be loved but often don't give that love to myself by connecting to the Spirit within. A brave new mourning requires that I look at what I really want. I have to be honest.

I am a person who wants to:

- Confidently live my life from a place of Divine Oneness—awake, alive, and loving, no matter the conditions I am experiencing
- Be present in my body and my life
- Bring out the best in myself and others and cultivate a compassionate understanding of the worst in myself and others

So how do I do, be, and have a brave new mourning, a new consciousness of grief?

- I surrender to each moment I'm in the "caterpillar soup."
- I ask for help, remembering I am not alone in grief.
- I choose my thoughts and act boldly to express my feelings.
- I accept the shifts within myself that ripple out to others as my world changes, and I am transformed.
- I appreciate the imaginal glimpses of my new self with grace and gratitude.

So what does a brave new mourning look, feel, and sound like? As a matter of fact, it is messy and exhausting. The old me turns to "soup" and the new me emerges, one image at a time, on a timeline beyond my knowing. Moments of discovery and curiosity support new thoughts on a river of ease. My mind calms as I am reminded that this grief is a gift. Self-care becomes a deepening of connection to that still, small voice within. I begin to trust myself more and more. I listen to my body and *all* the feelings within, allowing their rewiring. Meanwhile, I'm developing a new relationship with Reed through the principle of object permanence. Finally, I'm understanding and loving myself more deeply, as a conduit of light.

Can I stop making grief so hard?

Yes.

Am I willing to do that?

It's a question we each have to ask and answer for ourselves.

Discovering a New Thought with Curiosity

MARCH 1999

When I returned to Canada in March, the Synergy training deepened my experience of safety, security, and grounding. When my colleague Nan Elias and I hiked into the quiet, snowy woods one afternoon, my life would never be the same.

We were processing the benefits of the Synergy Method. Supporting our clients with touch, our presence and intention conveyed safety and security, allowing them to release the emotions of their stories and their old thoughts and then create new patterns of behavior. Sometimes the shift to a new perception, a new way of seeing things, occurs in an instant. But some clients may come to the table with an issue session after session.

Nan confessed, "I am just now getting comfortable with allowing myself to be supported. I'm more aware of choices I make that allow me to create that support for myself. Life does not have to be hard. In fact, it can be easy."

I froze on the path. "Wow!" I replied with awe. "What a concept: Support for myself. A life of ease."

"Yeah," she went on. "It has taken about a year, but I am now seeing support show up in the strangest places."

Without asking anything more, I replied, "I could use some support. Our business has virtually been closed by a powerful market trend. The government payment system has been revamped, and even large rehab companies that have been in business for years are closing." I sighed. "I feel so helpless once again."

"Well," she offered. "Set the intention that support can be drawn to you. Then just relax, and get out of the way."

The old idea and Midwest value of hard work leading to a good life had not been my experience in the fifth decade of my life. So it was that I was open to a brand-new idea. "I am not very good at relaxing, Nan," I told her. "I tend to believe I can do it all."

"Georgena, until you reprogram this belief that you are responsible for the world, you will be."

Just hearing Nan speak the word "support" aloud, my brain had changed the chemicals it was sending into my blood. I could feel my shoulders sink with ease as the idea of not being Hercules was released. In that moment, I realized that release, *real-ease*, was possible.

What a great idea for my Synergy clients.

Oh, wait, I thought to myself, *it is a great idea for me, too.*

The shift in my awareness had begun in the energy of this old-growth forest. Indeed, it was a place of "sacrodnicity": where synchronicity and the sacred intersect at the most opportune time.

Even with the gift of the beautiful, sacred mountain grounding me, I was still barely holding myself together. I had no understanding that my own belief was killing me—the idea that life had to be hard and I must carry the world on my shoulders. It was aging me dramatically.

I remember a lesson from Reed: *Being too hard on yourself can kill you.* I did not see that driving myself to do and be more was an incipient suicide. The "I have to make a difference" urge I could feel inside was really nothing more than my response to my deep-seated feelings of unworthiness.

I gazed at the pristine, diamond-encrusted snow that lay before me. Curiosity enfolded me.

Could my life possibly become one of ease? Could I become the Queen of Ease? I had opened to receive support early in my grief because I had to. Could I return to welcome it once again? Was it possible for me to lay down the "doing" as a Synergist and first be transformed by the method so I was truly available to my clients?

Nan and I arrived back invigorated for our next practice session as Synergy trainees. The beauty of this process lay in learning the "moves" to touch, listen, hold, protect, and facilitate releasing with our clients. We were practicing on one another. The trainee as client lying on the table was in the process of learning "to know thyself." She could experience firsthand the power of "Listening Touch." The trainee serving as Synergist was learning the method.

I was remembering that grief brings up the deepest parts of ourselves longing to be healed. And so, I asked first to be the client after we were paired up. I believed with all my heart that I could move through my grief, discover and integrate the estranged parts of myself, and live in that place of self-love and sacred service as a result. This belief was the "What" I wanted to have happen. In mere moments, I would show up to witness and experience the "How." The "Why" was my belief that we are all here on the planet now to simply love ourselves. Coming from that place of self-love, the entire planet would be different. Excruciating life pain would not be ended by the self-violence of suicide. Loving myself, my thoughts of self-loathing would cease.

"Relax into the table, Georgena. What are you noticing?" Kim was cradling my head in her hands.

"A pain in my right temple," I answered. I was so curious that there had been no pain until that moment. Then, spasms began shooting through my brain.

Kim Evans, a now a brilliant Synergist in Scottsdale, Arizona, supported my head firmly in her hands.

"A pain in your right temple. Does it have a size or a shape?"

"It is like a piece of black anthracite, exactly like my father's ashtray that was made out of shiny coal."

"A shiny black coal ashtray." Her fingers moved ever so slightly on the bony occipital ridge at the base of my skull. Silence allowed me to sink deeper into this embodied metaphor as I was safely held in her hands.

"It is heavy, Kim," I continued. "Beautiful to look at, but heavy to hold. Just like I am beautiful to look at, but all the stuff in my mind is heavy to hold."

"All the stuff in your mind is heavy to hold," she gently repeated. She moved down to my feet, touching them to ground me. This kept me in my body, connected to the sensations as well as the emotions of this unfolding story. I had not seen the ashtray while packing my dad's office. I wondered what had happened to it. My mind returned to the session.

"Yes," I said. "The critical voices cause me to doubt myself. They keep me super-responsible, on alert for what I need to 'fix.' All keep me so busy. I am tired, and I want to slow down."

"Critical voices causing self-doubt, being on alert for what needs fixing as the super-responsible, busy one."

"Yes."

"Tell me more about the On Alert, Super-Responsible one."

"I remember standing in the corner of the kitchen feeling the tension between my parents. I really felt afraid. They were both wonderful people but really different in their upbringing. Mother was from a Midwest farming family. Dad was from Pennsylvania. His dad was a coal miner who died of black lung disease. They were like oil and water, and, had they figured things out, they would have been such a great team.

"So I would try to send energy to calm things down. Or I'd come out of the corner and be cute to distract them."

"So you would feel the tension, either send calming energy or be cute to distract them."

"Yes."

"So where is that tension now?"

"In my head. In the form of the black lump of coal."

"So if this black coal had a voice, what would it say, Georgena?"

I felt a giggle burst from me. "Please Release Me," I began to sing.

Kim laughed and sang back, "Pleeeease Release Me."

And then, after a moment, I returned to the trance state, breathing deeply.

"Let the tension in your body go, Georgena," she gently commanded. "Lighten up and relax."

Even as a student, Kim was astute, not thrown off to follow the trail that felt good. She sensed the tension calling for release and brought me back to focus on it.

"So let me go," she repeated.

"Yeah." And then I began to shake all over. Kim looked up to catch the eye of Peggy Shaw-Rosato.

A Master Synergist, Peggy arrived with blankets that she piled onto me, placing her hand high on Kim's back to support her as the work deepened. We were all safe, supported, and grounded in the Method, every step of the training.

Sobs began to rack my body. The tension I'd held for nearly fifty years released in wave after wave for minutes on end. Nothing was said. This release needed no words, simply the Listening Touch and sacred space created by the Method, along with the well-trained staff.

Minutes later I was quiet. I could breathe even more deeply, sinking farther into the table, as the strain and stress of years of holding something not mine dissipated.

"So what is happening now, Georgena?" Kim inquired softly.

"I am seeing a lovely golden cord extend from the coal in my head to my heart."

"Tell me more," Kim requested.

"The coal is my fear. It is reaching out to be comforted by my heart." Kim repeated my words, skillfully deepening the experience as I listened to my deepest self.

"Tell me more," she said again.

This simple invitation or direction, depending on the tone of the Synergist's voice, provides the space to expand without interference or projections of the Synergist. I followed her guidance, empowered to continue. "The coal is afraid," I said. "It does not know how to be anything but busy. It is so tired of having so many projects going, so many incomplete lists, so many 'I have to dos.' It is really tired."

"So go back to the little girl in the kitchen, Georgena. What did she do when the tension between her parents increased?"

"Well she tried to fix it with her energy, and when that did not work, she twirled around, singing and dancing, which turned her dad's anger toward her instead of toward her mom."

"So she twirled around, singing and dancing, to distract her dad from being mad at her mom."

"Yeah," I concluded. "I guess that's what happened. I became very good at distracting others and myself." I felt my stomach twist and then relax, confirming this truth in my body.

I listen to this affirmation in my body, continuing to breathe and relax, as Kim gives me time to integrate this new "Aha."

"Distraction and busyness were patterns you developed as that twirling, singing, dancing little girl to ease the tension in your family. But that was then and this is now. So what are you noticing in your body right now?"

"I am feeling like a butterfly about to burst out of its cocoon,' I said.

"Tell me more."

"Well this insight is freeing. I can be like a quiet butterfly resting on a branch, just soaking in the sun or floating easefully on the breeze. I no longer need to rush here and there, over-commit, or distract myself to ease my tension."

"You can just be like an easeful butterfly," she affirmed.

Then I sensed Peggy as she stepped close to the table. Picking up my wrist she said, "Strong enough to fly thousands of miles like the monarch. Yet with fragile wings that make you vulnerable, gentle, and loving."

I opened my eyes slowly, feeling my head and shoulders. The pain in my head was gone. The weight was gone of being the busy fixer all my life. I was calmness, confidence, and conscious connection. I sensed the presence of my own self as well as these beautiful women. My addiction to busyness had been brought to light. *I* noticed—and it shifted. I could feel myself becoming lighter.

Now when the temptation arose to over-commit, I could choose from a place of power to bless, breathe in ease, and invite support into my life.

The grief of that little girl, of many years, was released as I walked out into the darkness. It would now be my privilege to serve as Kim's Synergist.

I am curious. What other ideas and beliefs about my life could be easily released and shifted by Synergy?

Why is it that Grief brings up the deepest parts of ourselves longing to be healed?

Discovering the Gift of Self-Care
MARCH 1999

"So how do you take care of yourself?" Ilana asked the class. "Most of you are here because you are very good as taking care of others. But do you really know how to listen to and care for yourself?" She went on to instruct us to close our eyes and notice the contact our bodies were making with our chairs, the wall behind us, or the floor beneath. She asked us to notice what was happening without judgment.

The room stilled, as if a lovely gossamer had enveloped us all. It held and enfolded us, allowing and supporting us to relax into deeper connection with body, breath, and heart. The presence of Spirit was clearly in the room as deep, easeful Peace.

I'd rarely surrendered deeply. I'd become a super caregiver. Falling into bed at night, exhausted from the day, or sitting in my prayer chair in the morning to welcome the dawn was the closest I'd come to this deep, easeful peace. And yet, peace had descended upon me the night of January 23, just before Reed failed the breath test. It was an unbidden gift of unconditional love. I now believe it was to show me two levels of my life that I would experience as I became open to loving myself by listening to the wisdom of my body.

The why, how, and when of Reed's soul would be revealed to me years later, when I was able to receive his messages.

It was also the felt sense of love that I could invite to live within me when I was willing to claim my worthiness.

During various trips to "get away from the grief" in Norfolk, we visited my brother Alan. Once he made the comment, "Do you realize how you're constantly waiting on Ed and Vincent? You ask them what they want to drink. After you get that, you ask them what you can fix them to eat." He got my attention the third time, when he pointed out my refilling their glasses before they asked.

I had not been aware of my addiction to caregiving. And yet in my family of origin, it was so important to do the things that got you noticed. You were loved because of what you did. My parents were astute at identifying and meeting the needs of those beyond the walls of our home. We frequently prepared meals for the ill or needy. Caring for others was truly one of our family values.

Giving to others without thought for myself had been what I'd heard from the pulpit since I was four years old. The second great commandment was, "Love your neighbor as yourself." Many sermons were preached on the "love your neighbor" part. But what about "as yourself"? I finally decided that I would request that Tom Guenther, our minister, preach a sermon to address that when I returned from this training module.

Ilana had designed our next training to teach us to be conductors of the session. We were not the composers. That role belonged to the client. Clients were often not aware of the freedom they had to write the score. Allowing time to arrive, settle, and breathe could prompt an issue from within the client that wanted to be voiced. Or, the client would show up ready to tell a story or relate an event. I learned to ask the question, "What would you like to have happen in our time together?"

Just as the conductor of an orchestra is aware of each instrument and the sounds it is creating, we as Synergists become aware of the client's breath, how he or she is lying on the table, if one shoulder is higher than the other, and myriad other details.

Ilana also called our attention to proper hydration, nutrition, exercise, and sleep as self-care tools. We learned to really listen to our bodies, moment by moment. We sought to know what was required to support ourselves during the many hours of lectures as well as the hour standing at the Synergy table.

Recently a client wailed, "How can I take care of myself when I am supposed to be missing my son?"

She assumed that by honoring and caring for herself, she was dishonoring her son. This was a myth that came to light. Her body, not me, gave her permission to pay attention to herself as a way of honoring the other. When she felt her shoulder sink into the table, she heard me repeat, "How can I take care of myself?" I felt her shoulder relax into my hand, and she noticed it was no longer up in the air. So it is that when this wisdom and guidance comes from within, it is felt by the body, and self-care is easier to choose.

I've become aware of my self-talk and its shift from ruthless critic to gentle or sometimes even hilarious guide. I've learned to ask the question, "What is the most kind and loving thing I can do, be, or have for myself in this moment?"

This has surfaced as an important self-care tool. It is a gift from me to me. It is not something I read in a book; it is just a clear question that showed up one day.

When asked often and with heartfelt curiosity, it points the way for me to self-care, then self-compassion, self-kindness—and eventually self-love.

Sometimes the answer is as simple as making myself a cup of hot water with a pinch of sea salt and lemon. Sometimes it is a time-out at work. After walking outside, circling around to another part of the nursing home, and breathing through my whole body, including my feet,

I enter the building once again, connected and aware—in just a few minutes.

This question is neither self-absorbed nor distracting. For in a place of ease, relaxation, love, and presence, everything and everyone around me responds with less fear and more openness, kindness, and love. But I must take *response-ability* to connect with myself. When I come from embodied awareness, I thrive as a human being in the Spirit of all there is.

This self-care thing is a lifelong, moment-by-moment process that I have said yes to, especially when I am serving others or when my critical self-talk emerges. It is like brushing my teeth. If I don't intentionally engage in self-care, I begin to give off a particular aroma. Smelling my bad breath is certainly not a treat.

Again I ask, "What is the most kind and loving thing I can be, do, or have for myself in this moment?"

When I feel my habitual patterns of pleaser, perfectionist, super-responsible-driven-doer emerging; when I feel stress gripping me or I feel overwhelmed, I simply remember to ask this question aloud and listen for the answer from within.

So clearly self-care is asking: "What is the most kind and loving thing I can be, do, of have for myself in this moment?"

1. A cup of tea? A glass of water with a pinch of sea salt and lemon?
2. A walk outside to feel my bare feet, with their 1,300 nerve endings per square inch, connect with the grass, the dirt, the sand?
3. One minute of peace and quiet as I turn away from the computer and stretch.
4. Being grateful for what I am doing, where I am or someone or something beautiful right in front of me?
5. Noticing my breathing. Exhaling like a lion and allowing a breath to come in. Counting the in-breath, pausing and then exhaling twice as long?
6. Going to the bathroom when I *first* feel the urge?

7. Feeling my hips in the car seat, the back supporting me, and placing my hands on an imaginary clock at four and eight on the steering wheel?

8. Befriending my body by asking someone to help carry or move something?

9. Reading a book?

10. Playing with a child?

11. Telling my story about Reed to a trusted colleague or family member?

12. Watching the clouds, trees, flowers, people outside the window?

13. As a feeling comes into my awareness, I now can stay with it. Notice it as if I were looking at a painting.

    (Just the other day, I came out of church on a gorgeous calm, sunny day in Portland, Oregon. Looking up into the cloudless sky, I felt sadness welling up in me. There was no man with whom to share this beauty and peace. I walked to my car. I sat inside and just allowed the sadness to envelop me. I let my tears be as I continued to breathe. No rush, no fear, just allowing. As suddenly as the sadness arose, after being witnessed for several minutes, it vanished. I wiped my cheeks, thankful I had not worn makeup, smiled for thirty seconds, and started the car, grateful for the tool of being present to my feelings and myself in this kind and loving way. No judgment. No mind spinning out of control this time. Just being with what was in the moment. Caring for myself.)

Listening Touch Supports Grief Release

JANUARY 2002

I look back at Ilana's teaching of Listening Touch, that very first training module. We sat in a big room with plush, pinkish carpet under our feet.

Ilana invited us to close our eyes and breathe deeply, slowly, simply, in and out. Then she invited us to imagine ourselves on a journey inside our bodies. As our attention moved from one part to the next, we were to notice which areas were calling for our attention. We might experience a sensation—tightness, ache, pain—or a particular place saying: "Stop and pay attention to me."

Once we discovered this place, we could simply float our hand onto it. If there were two places, we could use each hand, or if the hand placement was too awkward, we could imagine touching it.

We were then to focus on this area or areas, allowing the energy in our hands to flow freely. Our intention was clearly to *listen* to what this part of the body had to say, without analysis or judgment.

We were invited to begin a dialogue with this place in our bodies. For the truth is, each one of us on this planet is yearning to be listened to.

We imagined this particular part of the body with a voice. We asked, "What do you want to reveal to me?"

Listening from this place of intentional touch, we could actively hear the body's story. We were learning a powerful communicative tool. Each of us in the community was in the moment. We focused on what our bodies were saying.

At one point, my own body said, "I am so tired of holding myself together."

Truly, grief had broken me, turned me into caterpillar soup, and allowed me to glimpse God's imaginal cells of who I really was. Even so, my beliefs, habits, and patterns encased me like a Golden Buddha in a cement cocoon. It was the power of God and my intention to be love and light that kept me moving forward.

Ever listening, I continued to show up at the Synergy table.

It was one week before the fourth Reed's Day. I was attending a regional meeting in Arizona, where Melissa, a fellow trainee, accompanied me on my inner odyssey as a Synergist. Maddy served as gifted supervisor. The light filtered through the leafy trees outside, bathing our trio in beauty.

Melissa gently cupped her hands around my head, listening with unconditional love that flowed from her like a fountain. I felt the table beneath me, reminding me of the sands of my beloved Cannon Beach. My body sank into security. I felt ready to discover what images, feelings, and beliefs would emerge from the wisdom of my body, mind, and spirit.

"Georgena, what are you experiencing in your body?" she began. The question and her supportive touch allowed me to move deeper into my body.

"Tingly energy," I answered, "pulsing up and down the length of my left leg. I am surprised." Hearing my own words in the altered state of deep relaxation, an image fluttered through my mind. It was the surprise thirty-ninth birthday party Edward had orchestrated for me. Faces of beloved female friends at that party suddenly gave way to a new image, as I saw Reed being wheeled out of the garage, his face covered with a pristine white cloth shrouding the horror beneath it. It shocked my body into violent upheaval.

"Surprise is contrast, Melissa." I sobbed. "I'm experiencing the joyous surprise of Edward's women-only birthday bash and the unbelievable surprise of Reed's death."

My left leg began to shake as Melissa slipped her right hand under my hip and placed her left hand gently on the iliac crest above. "Tell me more about surprise, Georgena," she said tenderly, willing to go wherever that response in my left hip led.

"This grief is a surprise, I wailed. "I have been releasing this grief for four years. Where is all this sorrow coming from?" By now, cold energy was streaming from my body. Both of my legs were shaking. Maddy softly told Melissa, "Stay with the energy in the left leg. Follow it out, over and over."

"What are you noticing in your body, Georgena?" Melissa was fully present, using my name to keep me in touch with my body. She continued to touch my left hip, leg, and foot, over and over.

"I feel cold, like death. I'm freezing, and Antarctic snow stretches as far as I can see." Crying, I was the only person in this barren place. In that moment I was alone—until I felt Melissa's touch. *I am not alone. Ever.*

Suddenly, Maddy was tucking soft blankets around my entire stiff, cold body. I breathed. I felt myself begin to thaw. I simply stayed with the sensations of temperature in my body. I felt warmer.

Slowly, the image began to brighten to spring green. I was in my meditation meadow, warmed by the brilliant sunshine, comforted by the soft, lush grasses and red poppies. I was breathing deeply now.

"Where did that grief come from?" I asked now, walking down curiosity lane. No longer cold and afraid, I was present to my grief and could relate to it in a different way.

"It was held in your body, Georgena. Its release was triggered by the polarities of the word 'surprise.'" She paused. "What are you noticing in your body now?"

I took a very deep breath. Feeling the support of the table once again, I scanned my body. My right hip caught my attention, like a child waving to her teacher to be heard.

"My right hip wants to speak," I said.

"What would it like to say?"

"Let's explore the image that arose in me two years ago."

"Can you tell me more about that image?"

"It appeared around Labor Day during a Synergy session with Pam Hansen-Barnard in Sioux Falls. A convex sky electrified by millions of astonishing stars. I was looking up, filled with awe and delight. Right now, I'm situated in the very same sky, only it is concave. I'm being gifted by all I see."

"You are being gifted by all you see. Millions of astonishing stars fill you with awe and delight. Their light."

"Yes, Melissa. A powerful, peaceful, awesome feeling."

"Just let those feelings of power, peace, and awe expand through your entire body, Georgena."

And so, in the silence, I surrendered to this amazing scene. Every cell in my body opened to this profound spiritual reprogramming. I was in the Presence of Spirit.

Healing into wholeness in this moment of *whol-i-ness*, I was grateful for the courage in Melissa and myself to make this journey together. We had explored the divine expansive space of God within me.

Looking back on this immense grief release, I am aware that my mind was out of the way so that it could occur. My Inner Knower had come forth with the word "surprise" and the contrasting images. I had been in the space of timelessness, simply being, where the cells of my body could deeply, powerfully let go of their toxic tension.

My body was holding the pathway to reveal the healing image of the concave and convex stellar-verse initiated by Listening Touch so many years earlier. When it first appeared, I was not ready to fathom its mystery. I only knew it was an actual place—and significant. Like the mountain in my knee, it was there for my growth and support. I allowed that sky, for many years, to simply inhabit my right hip without trying to figure it out.

It is now clear that the stars in the sky above are my readers and the stars below are my audiences. All of you no longer want to have the dragon of Fragile Grief draggin' you around. You are those who want to be empowered to Intentionally Mourn and be transformed.

Sometimes we have everything required for our healing at our fingertips. We simply require the presence of another at the right time to support us with a word, a phrase, or a gentle Listening Touch so we can see, feel, and connect with the emotions to be released and the images within us.

Listening to yourself:

1. Think of something that makes you really scared, tense, angry, or sad.
2. Notice what is happening in your body.
3. Where are you feeling the tightness?
4. Does it have an image, a color, a sound, or a word?
5. Now rub your hands together until they feel warm.
6. Float them to that place in your body that felt tense just a minute ago.
7. Now think of that image, event, experience again that makes you feel scared, tense, angry, or sad.
8. Notice how you are feeling in your body with the support of your own gentle Listening Touch.

What is the difference when you have the support of touch?
You can do this the next time you are pulled down into the vortex of grief.

You may also locate a Synergist by going to:www.BefriendYourBody.org

Trusting Object Permanence

Thirty days after his departure, Reed had clearly communicated to me that his soul was soaring in the signature sunset. The swallowtail butterfly dipped so close to Edward in the spring of 1998 that he was able to scoop it up in his hand where it simply rested. Miss Alice, Reed's preschool teacher, told me her own story in March 1998.

Miss Alice and her assistant, Miss Cherry, had both lost children. They were standing in the parking lot after Reed's funeral service when Miss Alice saw a jet moving skyward. Its line of flight was straight up. "There he goes," she told Miss Cherry. It became a curiosity to notice when jets appeared, streaking straight across the denim blue and peony pink sunrises. It was as if Reed was saying, "Good Morning, Mom. You can't miss me!"

Other times, the line of flight is perfectly vertical, or the sign of an X in the sky. I smile, grateful. I felt this gratitude and delight whenever I received a photo via text from my dear friend Holly, in Colorado, sharing the joy of her world in the moment.

I've been asked, "But aren't these just natural occurrences that you are interpreting as signs from Reed?" When I first heard the question, I sat with it for months. The person who posed it was prominent in the Higher Consciousness Movement and had not lost a child or spouse. The question was asked from a very different life vantage point than mine.

It became clear to me that there were many, many things I missed during the day because my "Awareness Channel" was simply not attuned. Research has now discovered that we can only really be conscious of four words or two objects in the room at any one time. So in reality, we are living with only a hair's breadth of awareness. We miss so much. Not

117

because we do not care about all that is within and around us, but because of how our consciousness is currently functioning.

When one is in Raw Grief, one's brain is confused. Yet those on the other side do communicate with us. Oftentimes, we are overloaded and cannot take in any other information. At other times, those of us who have sunk into the vortex of grief hear and see a different world because of the "grief glasses" we are peering through. We are looking and listening for their communication to ease our pain of their absence in the physical body. We feel the separation from them. We can no longer hold them. We must wait for them to come to us and hold and hug us as we awaken from a dream in which their presence is palpable.

The signs started coming less frequently when I no longer needed constant assurances of his safety. I came to believe that my loved ones are like the mother in another room which I, the child can't see. Still there.

My longing for Reed began to shift when I began to trust that his Essence continued.

Which brings us to the question: *What relationship can we have with the soul of one who has left the body and departed?*

Each of us comes to our own understanding of this question. In his poignant poem, "The Essence of You," Don Cain came to a new relationship with his brother, John, who had passed. His brother became a joyous light in Don's life. The grief dissipated and Joy filled Don's heart.

The Essence of You

and I will pass the time fondly
for in your giving, I have received so very much
that your joy will carry forward ... even without a vessel
and its passage shall remain eternal and it shall see every shore
... such is the light you bring forth.

One of the most comforting things that arrived in the mail after Reed's passing was the poem, "Death is Nothing At All." I wish I could have met the author, Henry Scott Holland, for clearly he had a living, breathing understanding of the concept of object permanence. They are not gone; they have simply moved into another room out of our sight, away from our touch.

I knew early on that Reed had simply taken another form. Yet in all of this, a fear remained. I feared that others would forget Reed. There were many memorials to him: a garden on the cross country track at Skyview Lake in 1999, a bronze soccer player at the Tranquility Park Youth Soccer field in Omaha, and the stories I would still tell of him.

In July 2014, as I was writing this book, I received a call from Norfolk. It was my friend Kris Scheer. She wanted me to know that Reed's buddy Justin Web had gone to the cemetery. He discovered the eternal solar light was rusted and dark. On his own, he contacted the memorial company, ordered, and paid for a new one. Tears blur my vision now as I write these words. This birthday, July 27, 2014, Reed will have been on the other side for sixteen years—more years than he was a living, breathing human being. He is not forgotten.

A client recently shared: "They are not gone until nobody speaks their name."

Just this morning, I was talking to my friend Barb in Nebraska. We were comparing the weather in our respective worlds. Both Nebraska and Oregon weather are prone to drastic shifts, moment to moment. I said, "It is a clear morning here with a gorgeous pink, blue, and gold sunrise."

"A Reed sunrise," was her response.

She, too, remembered the first Reed sunset of denim blue and peony pink stripes, during the first thirty days after his passing. I'd recognized it myself this morning with its unique colors and design. His "Just checkin' in. I love you!" message.

From the very beginning, I was admonished, "Don't hold on." I did not feel that I was. My curiosity prompted the questions: *Did you leave too soon, Reed? What are you doing now?*

Remarkably, I had people approach me from time to time and ask if I had lost a child. They had seen a young man standing beside or behind me. They clearly were getting Reed's messages.

In my early Fragile Grief, I was angry that I could not see him or hear him when this happened. Once again, my anger was directed at me and at what I imagined was "wrong" with me. I simply did not realize that he and the person who experienced him were on a different frequency than I was. I was on the HBO channel, while Reed and the viewer were on Public Broadcasting. It was as simple as that. In time, my own ability as a medium evolved, and now the departed often appears at the Synergy table with a message for my client—a beloved mother, son, or spouse. This visit from the other side is simply the departed stepping back over into the room—our Earth—for the moment, with a message of love.

So it is with great gratitude that I recall Dr. Piaget's concept of object permanence to dissipate the anguish of longing and allow heart and mind space to be filled with love. The gift of object permanence becomes an even greater blessing, enriching my life, so that I may continue to fly into a New Mourning.

Now What?

———————— 🙡 🙞 ————————

Now, my relationship with Reed expands as I grow into the peace of being the Trauma Specialist and Grief Guide that I am today. It was his gift to me. I teach Mindful Grieving and Intentional Mourning so that we as a nation can truly be brave as we move into the vortex of grief—and free as we move beyond our grief.

The clients who come to the Synergy table are here because they do not want to walk through their grief alone.

One woman recently came to confirm that there was nothing lingering before she began a new relationship. She wanted to explore those deepest parts of herself, longing to be healed, that her Fragile Grief brought up. I admired her desire to show up clear for a new beloved. How often do people enter the dating world without doing their work, still in love with another? Still grieving the one that is no longer present, the new relationship cannot be built on a solid foundation clarity, trust, and love.

Many clients show up not realizing they are still in grief. They believe that their anxiety, shoulder pain, or depression is something unrelated to grief. They do not connect their awakening each night at 2 a.m. to grief. So I help them assess whether grief is affecting their lives, I guide them to identify its effects, and I teach them self-care tools to help them move beyond their grief.

These clients gift themselves with a Synergy session, discovering a tool to teach them to return to their bodies and listen to the still voice within. It may be, for example, a stabbing pain in the heart that evolves into an image of a golden light and then a message, "You are safe."

It may be an image in the body that gives them permission to begin a new chapter in their lives. One woman saw a Halloween costume that she had made for her now-departed son. She glimpsed the new career as a designer that emerged from her hip and celebrated this freedom to fully live once again. The body tells the truth and reveals our deepest wisdom.

So what do you want to have happen with your Raw, Fragile, or Gentle Grief?

I invite you to employ the tools of curiosity, self-care, listening to your body and its messages, and object permanence when you are ready to move into and through your grief. Please know that there is nothing wrong with you, wherever you are in this moment.

I had a man send a scathing e-mail after reading the description of my Grief Relief Workshop. In it, people learn to recognize where grief lives in their bodies by naming it. They are then given resources: the tools of breath and grounding to go down into the vortex of grief to discover where it lives in their bodies. They claim they have grief. Then, by releasing one thought that is keeping them stuck in grief, they tame it. He had read that having grief meant that there was something wrong with him and that this workshop would "fix" it. I simply sent him loving compassion that in this moment. We were just not on the same wavelength. I was on PBS and he was on ESPN.

Thank you for joining me as one of the many who have brought grief out into the light. Blessings all over as you continue on your life journey.

Glossary

Anticipatory Grief: Anticipatory grief refers to an experience of **grief** before an impending loss. Typically, the impending loss is a death of someone close due to illness, but it can also be experienced by dying individuals themselves. **Anticipatory Grief** may or may not result in a less intense and prolonged grief journey.

Mindful Grief: Mindful Grief is the process of 1) recognizing the many facets of grief (feelings, physical, mental, and spiritual) 2) feeling, listening to, and experiencing the dissipation of fear using Listening Touch 3) Exploring the tools of curiosity, discovery, object permanence, and self-care as supports to move through and beyond grief.

Grief: Grief is the internal state of deep, dark, anguished feelings, thoughts, and beliefs that live in the body and are a natural consequence of loss.

Grief Stages:

Raw Grief: Typically the first ninety days or less after the loss, when the brain is in a state of shock, confusion, and disorientation. You feel raw, as if you have no skin. You experience crying nonstop and disrupted sleep and eating patterns and wonder if you are going crazy. It feels as though grief has spilled over the tapestry of your life, covering everything. Grief is being 'done to you'. You feel like a victim.
Animal associated with Raw Grief: Coyote (Wailing is healthy.)

Fragile Grief: Sadness, anger, and loneliness that may last for months, years, or the rest of your life if you do not go down into the vortex of grief, feel where grief lives in your body, lean into it, and learn from it. It feels as though grief is a thick, heavy rope that is running through the tapestry of your life. You continue to feel like a victim.

Animal associated with Fragile Grief: Dragon (It is draggin' you around.)

Gentle Grief: Returning to the aliveness, happiness, and joy of life. You have discovered the gifts in grief and reinvented yourself, and you continue to honor your departed.

Animal associated with Gentle Grief: Deer (Quiet; the doe does not attack.)

Impulsicide: Ending one's life impulsively because the unbearable pain in the moment supersedes plans for one's future.

Intentional Mourning: Emoting the deep, dark, anguished feelings emerging as grief through wailing, crying, sobbing, or expressing emotions in the presence of others or in solitude. Selecting self-care strategies to move through grief in the healthiest possible process.

Listening Touch: Intentional touch of a Synergist as the client tells his or her story and the emotions and constrictions of the body due to this invasive trauma are released. Individuals can be taught Listening Touch to connect with their bodies and their messages, sensations, and emotions.

Resources

Having trouble sleeping? Go to:
http://www.beyondyourgrief.com/grief-counseling-services/products/

To find a Synergist near you, go to:
http://www.befriendyourbody.org/

About the Author

Georgena Eggleston, MA, trauma specialist and grief guide, became a complicated griever after burying the bodies of her brother, father-in-law, mother, father, and teenaged son in three and a half years.

After discovering where grief lived in her body through the Rubenfeld Synergy Method®, Georgena continued her deep personal work and became a certified synergist. Knowing we will all experience grief, Georgena teaches mindful grieving and intentional mourning so people have the tools to move beyond their grief. She is the mother of two sons and loves yoga, flower arranging, entertaining friends, and dancing. Georgena lives in Portland, Oregon.

Contact Georgena at: www.BeyondYourGrief.com or email her at: georgena.eggleston@gmail.com. Subject line to read: A New Mourning

CPSIA information can be obtained
at www.ICGtesting.com
Printed in the USA
FFHW02n1610201018
48894425-53122FF